The Secret Life of an Astral Traveler

Adventures Out of Body for Healing and Romance

by

Luna Star Van Atta

Luna Star Van Atta
Moon Dancer Productions, LLC
Visit my website at www.lunavanatta.com

Printed in the United States of America
First Printing June, 2016
Published by Sojourn Publishing, LLC

ISBN:978-1-62747-220-3
Ebook ISBN: 978-1-62747-221-0

Dedication

With Divinely-inspired gratitude, I dedicate this book to my husband, Michael Van Atta, who resides on the other side of the veil. As I sat at the keyboard, his words streamed forth and appeared on the screen. His name should probably be on the cover of this book as the author. The writing of this book actually began in 2003 about eight months after my husband and I first met. Together, we had profound experiences in the astral planes and wanted to write a book that would touch the lives of others; helping invalids, the elderly, prisoners, etc., to realize that they could expand their lives beyond the confinements and restrictions of the three-dimensional world.

As I did research for the book, I found many of the emails that my husband and I sent to each other about the book we had planned to write together. Here is an excerpt from one that Michael wrote to me on December 31, 2002.

I awoke from a dream in which my spirit guides said I was to write a book from information that they would channel through me. The beings from the other side, beings who already held the book in their hands, told me, "Just open a file on your computer and we will put into your mind the words you are to say. We will read from the book that we are holding and pass the words onto you telepathically, we will put them into your consciousness and you will do the typing. Your job is to keep up!"

As I now read this email it is as if Michael is saying those words to me from the other side of the veil.

Michael started bits and pieces of the book back then but soon after he received his first cancer diagnosis and our lives together changed quickly and the book was forgotten until now.

From the other side of the veil, thirteen years later, Michael dictated this book to me, and I added some of my own information. The book finally is birthed. Without Michael in my life, I would have continued to hold a very important and very secret part of my life closely to me.

Michael knew that it would be a good thing to spread the word to others and help them move past the obstacles in our physical lives that hold us captive. The truth is that we all have the ability to travel beyond the physical world and to experience the realms of the angels and spirits.

We knew that we could write a book that would open up new worlds for people on our planet. Our book would help them rise above the self-imposed restrictions of our material world.

All of the journal entries and emails shared here, although of a personal nature, were agreed upon by Michael and me to be included in this book. It is a sharing of intimate details of our lives to serve the greater good.

Words of Gratitude

This book would not exist if it were not for the encouragement of many friends, clients and relatives who cheered me on and got excited about the final product. Many times I missed a yoga class or a drumming circle or rescheduled a client or other event so I could focus on this book. I feel special gratitude for my new love and soulmate, James Casey; my daughter, Jennifer Whitford; special friends Barbara Sheridan, Vishali Shahin, Sophia Garrett, and Mary Funkhouser who all stood by me as I needed their patience while I completed my writing; Karen Koebnick, who opened doors for me in birthing my new career; as a speaker; my spiritual mentor Michael Mirdad; my Reiki Master Teacher Jim Reigle; Tom Bird, book whisperer and his assistant, Mary Stevenson for all of the mentoring and emotional encouragement; the Beta 2 Charlie Coyote Group who never gave up on me; Rama Jon for his guidance, keeping me always focused on the next step; and my Remote Viewing peers: Gary Beavers, Michael Bonnett, Lance Beem and Wendy Fickbohm. Everyone in this support group either encouraged me, had patience with my time restrictions, or mentored me in some way to make this book a reality. To all of you I send love from my heart to yours.

Table of Contents

Introduction

*"If you are going to be weird,
be confident about it."*
Author unknown

*"The only obligation in any lifetime is to be true to yourself.
Being true to anyone else or anything else is not only
impossible, but the mark of a fake messiah."*
"Illusions, The Adventures of a Reluctant Messiah."
Richard Bach

Born on February 18th at 11:57 p.m., I landed on the cusp of Aquarius and Pisces, destined to live two different lives as if I were two souls occupying the same body. By day, I worked in the conservative industries of oil and gas and later insurance. Putting on business suits, pantyhose and heels and working long hours under high stress, I lived the analytical, material life of the business world. Nights and weekends, I relaxed into my true life's calling; astral traveler, Remote Viewer and alternative healer. For more than thirty years I kept a large part of my life private from even some of my closest friends.

This book is a healing for the two halves of myself to integrate and make amends with each other so I can embrace a healing of One-ness. This book is also a labor of love and therefore, effortless.

The very first event that made me realize I was being "groomed" by God for great things occurred when I was just a child. Extensive dental work meant long hours in the chair and I was already acutely aware that having another human so intimately connected to my energy field was not something I was comfortable with. As it turned out there was an elementary school across the street from the dentist office with a nice selection of swing sets. This particular dentist was slow and meticulous. Each appointment seemed to last for hours. To cope with the invasion of the dentist into my energy field, I would astral travel although I did not know what it was called at that time. Feeling that I had to escape from the dentist who was invading my space, I left my physical body and sent my spirit across the street to swing with the other children until the dentist was done. As a very young girl I realized I could leave any environment that did not make me happy. I could take a mini recess, enjoying life until it was time to return to my body. This new ability was enlightening.

Later on, when I was sixteen, I was lying on my back on my bed staring at the ceiling and listening to Jefferson Airplane's "Surrealistic Pillow" on a 33 and 1/3 RPM album. I apparently achieved an altered brain wave state. My spirit popped out of my physical body abruptly. *Oh my God, oh my God, oh my God!!!!* It was like a falling dream that startles you awake, except that I was "falling up." It was so very scary.

And then, as quickly as I popped out, I popped back in. I laid there, afraid and stunned. This was a life-changing event for me. Suddenly I was a new person. The big lesson I learned that day was that my emotions and thoughts were stored in my energy field, not in my physical body. The physical body was just a shell; no intelligence or emotions were left behind when I projected up and out of my body. This was a profound lesson for me, as I was raised to believe that the physical body was everything. What we interacted with each day and what we talked with and walked with and put food in was who were truly were. My parents were WASPs; white Anglo Saxon Protestants. They knew nothing of the spirit world and in fact I did not know of anyone that I could speak with about my strange adventure. I did not have any friends or relatives that I knew of who had similar experiences. And of course, no one knew that I had this experience because I certainly would not share the information with anyone. In fact, this adventure was something I would not share with anyone for more than forty years.

I questioned if it actually happened at all. I laid on my bed stunned, thinking that maybe I had just experienced a strange dream of some sort. But the following week, it happened again. Now I believed it. This was my beginning of exploring the etheric realms.

After those two events, I began to hear my deceased grandmother, Vera, speaking to me through the radio. I made the inappropriate decision to share that with my parents, who immediately retreated into a stance of fear and sent me to a psychiatrist. Unfortunately, our society fears such closeness to God and the world of the angels. It is more acceptable to place many layers of clergy between us and the Divine. Our society teaches us at a very young age that any out-of-body experience is a sign of non-conformity or even worse, mental illness. We just need to re-learn what is possible and embrace that closeness to God. It is our Divine right to be One with the Creator and within that relationship, to embrace all that is offered.

There have been other strange occurrences in my life, many of which are shared in this book. Meeting my husband, Michael, was one of them. He was a unique person and not only accepted my strange life but also brought his own strangeness to the relationship.

As I look back on all of the interesting and unique threads, as they were assembled together, wove a fabric that detailed my life's purpose: helping others become familiar and comfortable with death and the other side of the veil. Although I have had some unique experiences, it also became clear to me that all of humanity has the ability to experience the other side of the veil.

Much of my adult life I have experienced the astral planes. This is an environment where emotions are intensified as they fold over upon themselves with all of time. Here, past, present, and future are experienced simultaneously.

Due to client confidentiality and other issues that prevent me from divulging some specific information, I have changed some names in this book; however the facts remain the same.

One

For Whom the Bell Tolls

*"I stared at the beautiful Being of Light who shimmered
before me. He was like a bagful of diamonds emitting a
soothing light of love.Any fear I might have had at the
notion of being dead was quelled by the love
that poured from the Being before me."*
"Saved by the Light." by Dannion Brinkley

Dream September, 2012.
Twenty-two Months Before Michael's Death
*Michael and I are getting ready to go on a trip.
When we get to the airport we are late and the
plane has already pulled away from the elevated
tunnel platform. They make an announcement on
the loud speaker, calling us by name and saying
we are to walk out to the runway and that they
are holding the plane for us. When we get there
the plane has pulled up next to a tree. We are
supposed to climb the tree to board the plane.
Michael scrambles up the tree and gets into the
plane. I am trying to climb the tree, but the
branches are not substantial enough even though
I weigh less than he does. They keep bending over,
returning me to the ground.*

1

While this is happening, John Lennon and Yoko Ono walk by and John says, "Jesus Christ, look what they are making us do now!" I go into the airport and try to call Michael. His cell phone is off because he is on the plane. I go back out to the runway and try to climb the tree again. I realize I am trying to hang onto a newspaper while I am climbing and it is hindering progress. I get rid of all the advertisements and fold up the rest of the paper and put it in my purse.

Now I can't find my ticket. So I go through the newspaper to see if the ticket got folded up in it. I did not find it and then feeling fully frustrated, I wake up.

Dream Interpretation
September, 2012

Michael is called to death, to the etheric realms. I want desperately to go with him. It is an easy ascent for him. No matter how hard I try, my frequency is too heavy to ascend at this time. John Lennon, (who later in 2014 becomes one of my healing guides) enters the dream to give me support. I cannot reach Michael by cell phone because he is in a different energetic frequency. Then I think that if I can remove myself from my material life (advertisements), that I will be able to ascend. Then I think the reason that I cannot ascend is because I am too attached to the negative messages that are published by the media (newspaper). Even with these adjustments, I am still not able to find my ticket and so I am not able to leave. Feeling great frustration about being stuck in the three-dimensional world while Michael is able to ascend, I wake up.

The dream was a premonition. Over the previous twenty- two months, Michael and I had laughed about my interpretation of the dream: that he would make an easy transition when the time was right and that I would be left behind due to lessons I still needed to learn about materialism and negativity (the advertisements and the newspaper) and that my energetic frequency (the weight that kept bending the branches) was not high enough. I would be left behind.

Now here I was, July 27, 2014, standing in our dining room, next to the hospice place that was placed there the previous day. I was watching as my husband was getting ready to ascend and my guides told me I was to help with the transition. My spirit guides were urging me to assist his spirit to leave his body. I knew I was capable of making that happen without leaving evidence behind. Helping a spirit leave a body is less obvious than a physically-assisted death. This would be an invisible process. Who would know?

Watching the life force draining from his body was torturous. I sensed his spirit teetering on the edge between life and death. My heart tugged on me to somehow make him stay. My spirit guides said to release him. I heard song lyrics playing somewhere in the ethers: "*Don't fear the reaper, we'll be able to fly, we can be like they are, come on, baby, take my hand, don't fear the reaper, baby I'm your man."* I believed that leaving the earth plane with him was the best solution for me, I wanted to follow him into the light. He was dying; I could go with him. I wanted it more than anything I had ever wanted. He was my twin flame. We had been reunited in this lifetime to make this world a better place. We had done much work in the astral planes together and now it was time for him to leave. Permanently.

I was to be left behind. I was not to just allow him to go; now I was to help him leave. I was to assist him in the dying process. This was a clear and focused demand from my spirit guides.

Help him die!.... Oh, I felt so overwhelmed. How was I supposed to hold myself together and embrace the role of the ultimate healer; a healer who assists in returning the spirit to God. I could not just be a grieving widow, I was to help my husband die.

Assisting a loved one to die is an old debate, one that we humans have grown tired of. At what point in time will we be able to legally assist our terminally ill with the transition into death? After all, we do that for our pets. Our canines and felines are honored with those decisions. But we humans are supposed to sit back and watch our loved ones suffer and watch their physical bodies deteriorate without helping them move along in a timely manner.

Michael had certainly experienced physical discomforts. Fighting cancer for more than ten years, he was finally giving in and getting ready to meet God.

His physical body was preparing to release his spirit, a spirit I knew intimately. It was one I had spent an extraordinary twelve years with in the spirit world. Together we had accomplished more Remote Viewings and astral adventures than we could count. Now he was getting ready to leave and return to the spirit world. Michael and I, as twin flames who found each other late in life, had accomplished exceptional things in more than a decade that we savored together. We spent much of our marriage out of our bodies, spirits merging; doing work in the astral planes. We had our own amazing intimate interactions as well as astral work that benefited the lives of others.

Michael had not eaten for eleven days. We knew the time had descended upon us. The dogs knew it too. They were restless. Three times they ran to the front door and barked. No physical person was visible each time I opened the door. Maybe Michael's relatives were arriving from the other side to help with his transition.

Staying focused on the important task in front of me, I solicited the help of my dear sister-in-law. "Come on Ann, your brother is getting ready to go. I need you to help me anoint him and hold the energy in this space."

Ann had been fervently praying the rosary with a rocking motion that was intense and sending out waves of energy into the space. The mantra provided her with comfort in this emotional and energetically chaotic experience of her brother's transition.

My Reiki Master Teacher, Jim Reigle, had called from Show Low, a small town in northern Arizona. He was on his way to our home to conduct an End-Of-Life Ceremony for Michael and assist him in the transition. Now, Jim and I both knew that he would not have time to arrive before the silver cord detached from Michael's physical body, allowing the spirit to ascend. Jim described the ritual to me over the phone, a process that would encourage Michael's spirit to vacate the physical body and permit the silver cord to disconnect.

Now, only Ann and I would take on that responsibility.

If anyone had been watching they would have seen Ann and I, both Reiki Masters, holding our hands in specific positions, using sacred symbols and breath work while applying essential oils as we moved around Michael's body. On the etheric planes there was so much more happening. I was working on the chakras; the seven major energy centers that align down the center of the body; closing some, opening others. There was communication taking place between our spirit guides and Michael's spirit readying him for the transition.

"Stay focused, stay focused!" I used some self-talk to try to hold myself together. My husband was dying. I could be the emotional wife who was losing her twin flame, or I could take on the role of the Reiki Master healer and do this important work. Stepping up to the role of healer, I allowed my spirit to release control of my physical body as I had done hundreds of times before when doing

Reiki healings. I allowed God energy to move in and use my body to liberate Michael's spirit. I moved my spirit body to the side and placed it in the corner of the room; doing my best to stay out of the way. Source used my hands to draw the sacred symbols. We applied carefully chosen essential oils in specific places. Breath work, intention, focus were all incorporated into the ceremony while at the same time I relinquished control.

Within my Reiki practice, I had facilitated many healings but had assisted in this very intimate level of transitioning a spirit only a handful of times. And this time it was not just any spirit, it was that of my husband.

The seriousness of the event weighed heavily upon my emotions. I knew that many times it's difficult for a spirit to leave if loved ones have an emotional hold on them. *Help him leave, keep your emotions out of it.* It was not my intent to make it more difficult for him to leave. That energy would hold him in place in the physical world to suffer longer. I did my best to remain a clear channel for God energy to come in and work through me.

My spirit guides surrounded me and guided me through the process. The essential oils chosen resonated with the unique frequencies of each of the chakras. As Ann and I did the work, the mixture of Michael's energy centers combining with the essential oils were communicated to my brain as colors, beautiful strobing colors of light. Filled with the Bliss of Source, the sacred Reiki symbols appeared as holograms as I moved through the chakras, beginning with the root chakra located at the base of the spine and methodically moving upward, ending at the crown chakra at the top of the head. I silently chanted specific prayers and kept reminding myself to keep my heart out of the process so I would not make it harder for him to leave. I encouraged my husband's energetic spirit body to move up and out through his crown chakra.

I felt Michael's eyes on us. Right now he was probably looking down on us from a vantage point of a mile. I imagined that he probably could not hear me but I was still drawn to look up toward his spirit body and say to him, "Oh honey, I am going to miss you so much. What an extraordinary relationship we had. You introduced me to a life beyond limitations. We were a Divinely-inspired team. Now you are free to move forward and to be one with God and I so wish I were going with you!"

A unique individual, Michael was a man directly connected to God and the energies of the spirit world. Through the twelve years I knew him he opened my eyes and my heart to possibilities and a limitless life of incredible experiences. Together we became Reiki Master Teachers, accomplished important Remote Viewings and facilitated many miracles that God worked through our hands.

Ann and I completed our End-Of-Life Ceremony. Slipping back into my body I recognized a bonding of energy between me and my dear sister-in-law as sisters in the etheric realms. The gift we gave her brother was one that few will ever experience. Our eyes met and exchanged a deep inner knowing. We had completed our ritual. It was an expression of deep love for her brother and my husband.

"Now we wait," I said softly. We sat down to let the energy settle in. Sitting next to the hospice bed, we focused on reintegrating back into the three-dimensional world. The contrast of leaving The Bliss of God we had experienced during the ceremony with settling into the reality of the physical space was worse than being trapped in a dentist's chair. A cloak of dread enveloped me. The life-changing enormity of what was taking place swallowed me up. I sat down and tried to get my head around the complicated and mixed energies and emotions that were swirling through the room. Anxious, sad, elated, full of wonder, love, loss....so many feelings flooded my heart. I was elated for him. I was devastated for me. My right arm was being amputated. This man who altered my life, who taught me how to love with the depths of God's love, was leaving me.

As I fully integrated back into my physical body I was assaulted by the sound of Michael's labored breathing. It was so difficult to hear the gasps of air, as his lungs did not know how to discontinue the work they had done for sixty-six years sustaining Michael's physical body. The erratic breaths spread out farther and farther apart, separated by long agonizing voids of silence. I realized I was focused on that wheezy, labored breathing. I was mindlessly counting the agonizing seconds between each gasp for air, wondering how long it would be before silence would offer its sad relief to this process. I teetered on the edge of insanity.

We needed a break from the irritating sound of the breath gasping, wheezing, moving in and out of his lungs in irregular patterns, long pauses in between each breath. An earth shattering gasp breaking the silence and then waiting, waiting..... waiting.......I found myself holding my own breath within each silence. *"Is this the last one?"* And then another gasp would be expelled rocking my world with an earthquake of sound. The experience of waiting for each chaotic breath felt haphazard and out of the natural flow of life. The gasping reminded me of a time when I was a child trying to save fish that were flopping around in shallow pool when a higher level of water had subsided. It was a desperate feeling and this time there was nothing I could do to save the one who was floundering.

"Let's sit out on the patio" one of us said to the other... I can't remember who thought of it.

The backyard was still. Six sets of wind chimes hung quietly in anticipation from my patio eaves. There was a comforting silence in the air. We sat out there, talking about Michael and what a unique individual he was. Not just as a husband and brother and father but also as a healer, Remote Viewer, teacher, Vietnam veteran, undercover spy searching for forgotten POW's, and spiritual leader. Michael took all of his roles in this lifetime seriously.

After a while I stood up and took a deep cleansing breath way down into my lower abdomen, collecting my stamina. My turn to go in and check on Michael.

My heart asked, *Will he still be breathing?* I walked in listening with anticipation. Silence. I felt dread pour over me like nasty black motor oil. What if I have to walk outside and tell Ann that her brother is dead; permanently dead? I listened. There was a long pause...then I heard the GASP! It rocked my existence. *It's not time yet.* I did my best to disconnect my energy from Michael's. After sleeping together, making love, accomplishing healings together, astral traveling, remote viewing... all of the extraordinary experiences that connected our energies over the years; now I needed to just disconnect and release him to God.

I sat with him for a few minutes and pushed the strained words out of my constricted vocal cords. "It's okay, honey, you can leave. I love you and I know you are ready to have the Big Adventure. I wish I could be with you!" I could feel his energy signature around me and within me. It was a good feeling; a feeling of love and anticipation. I sat for a few minutes, my face contorted with mixed emotions. I said a prayer and thanked God for bringing Michael and me together.

I heard Michael's spirit send me the message, *"It's okay, I will still be with you, watching over you and I will be one of your spirit guides, helping you from the other side. We will form a direct conduit of communication between your world and mine."*

I knew before long he would be looking down on me and his empty shell of a body. He would be released of the burden of the terrible illness he had been dealing with for ten years. In fact I felt that he was probably already suspended above his physical body watching me.

As I walked back outside, Ann and I locked eyes. Her eyebrows raised, her look was a mixture of anticipation and dread. I cast my eyes downward with a gentle shake of my head which sent her the silent message: *It's not time yet.* There was no need for words to convey the current status. We sat and chatted some more about Michael, feeling the comfort of being together through this difficult challenge.

Suddenly one set of wind chimes began ringing loudly. Not all of the six sets of wind chimes that surrounded the patio....just one set! *That's interesting!* Ann and I looked at each other and released some of our tension with laughter. Was this a message from Michael? This is exactly the type of thing he would do. An element of surprise and delight to pull us from our grief. Had the energy of his spirit body leaving the physical been able to send us this message; ringing the bells to let us know it was his time?

We went back into the house together. Silence. No breathing. We wait. Still no breathing. Ann walked over to Michael and in an otherworldly voice the words "he's gone!" were ejected from her. Her tears flowed. Tears of relief, tears of regret, tears of closure. Tears of wanting. Tears of wishing for one last conversation; one last hug or smile.

Somehow, I had no tears. Maybe because I knew from my history with death that he was experiencing total bliss. I knew Michael was probably already merging with God. I knew this from my own death that happened during surgery in Wheat Ridge, Colorado in 1984. I was not aware of the exact time the silver cord disconnected but I felt Michael's energy moving away from me.

This moment with my husband was one of many that have been etched into my heart, although this was possibly more intimate than any other. Assisting a loved one with a deathing process is much like assisting a new life coming into this world. The deathing process resembles the birthing process; a transition into an altered state of consciousness. The difference is that when a new life is coming into the physical world we are full of hopes and dreams for their new life. It evokes certain emotions in us that fill our hearts with joy. Assisting with a death of a loved one, helping their spirit to leave their physical body, is a more difficult process. They are moving into a life without you. In this case, my heart was filled with love but there was an ominous heaviness at the same time.

I knew from my own personal Near Death Experience that his spirit body would leave the physical body through the crown chakra. I also knew that the silver cord has no intention of disconnecting until it is ready. It would stay connected until he reached that turning point when the silver cord would break and his spirit would ascend.

Michael was surrendering into the full-blown experience of death – what some think of as so final. It is an event that I truly look forward to experiencing. I know it is only one event on the timeline of my energetic body's experience through many lifetimes. My Near Death Experience had given me the knowledge of what he was now enjoying. I knew from my prior experiences that Michael was moving toward The Bliss.

How long would it be before Michael would transition his spirit body into another physical body? I had no idea.

A couple of weeks later, I did receive communication from Michael that he was in classes, an Astral University of sorts and working directly with Ascended Masters. This did not surprise me, as Michael was an evolved being.

I thank God I was able to help Michael with his transition. My Near Death Experience had been a training session to prepare me for this significant event.

While looking through files to do research for this book I ran across a copy of the wall calendar page for April, 2014, three months before his death, scrawled across the top in very large red sharpie letters, Michael had written "THANK YOU HOLY SPIRIT." Knowing that his death was imminent, he was expressing gratitude for God allowing him to celebrate his sixty-sixth birthday on April 29, 2014.

Two
Initiation as a Delog

*"Astral projections have been described in Egypt, India, China and Tibet from pre-historic times. In Tibet the phenomena were so frequent that those who produced them were given a special name - **Delogs** - meaning 'those who return from the Beyond'.*
"The Key of Solomon The King. (Calvicula Salomonis) 970-928 BC,"
translated by S. Liddell MacGregor Mathers

Dying, meeting with God, and having a second chance to live my life left me a changed person. I transitioned overnight from being a materialistic party girl to becoming deeply spiritual. When I left my body during surgery that went bad, I was groomed to do great things and meeting Michael was part of God's plan for that to take place.

When I left my body in 1984, my spirit slipped out of my physical body through the top of my head, much like a hand slipping out of a glove. It was effortless. It happened without any thought. Suddenly I was suspended above my body. A feeling of being vacuumed up into the silence. My astonishment gave birth to the thought: *"Oh, I must be dying! Who would have thought that was going to happen!?"*

My spirit quickly soared above my physical body. With 360-degree vision, I saw my physical body below me as slightly more than one inch long lying on the hospital bed. The bed reminded me of a boat floating aimlessly in an ocean of nothingness. I could see the hospital staff rushing around my lifeless body, which lay on the white sheets. The vision reminded me of parasailing in Mexico. A rope tethering me to the boat; now it was my silver cord that tethered me to my physical body. I must have been up pretty high for my body to look so small and inconsequential. I was aware that the hospital staff was injecting the body with something but had no physical feeling of that happening. Able to see through the floors and ceilings of the hospital, there were no obstructions to my vision. As I floated upward I watched the chaos that unfolded below me. I had no sense of the sounds or the emotional energy that was taking place, only the vision of the scene as if watching TV with the mute button pushed. Within my space of tranquility, I could hear nothing of the shouting and the frantic movements that I was watching.

They were racing to save my life. Why? It all seemed so meaningless. Why remain in a physical shell that I was not committed to. I didn't care if they succeeded. I was entirely disconnected. In fact I did not even feel that I owned that little body down there. It was just a thing that had been cast aside, like an old shoe. It was not part of me.

How could it be that my spirit had been housed in that physical body just moments before and now I didn't feel that I had ever had a connection to it? This epiphany just reinforced events that had happened previously in my lifetime and now here was another confirmation that the true REAL me was the spirit, not the physical body.

As I hovered and looked down at the cast-off body, I was feeling only wonderment and amusement about the experience. It was almost comical to realize that the 3-D world places so much importance on saving a physical body when it is not really who the person is. Why is it that the physical body holds so much importance to those who are in it? We dress it up and obsess over it and define ourselves by it, when in reality it is truly the energetic, spiritual body that holds all of the information of who we are. All of the thoughts and feelings and experiences are truly stored in the spirit body, not the physical body. Yes, the energetic body can have an impact on the health of the physical body over time. Our energy signature contains all of our past, present and future lives; it is who we truly are. I had no investment in the outcome of the diligent efforts of the hospital staff; I was neutral and detached. What happened next was truly life changing.

I was now approaching the light. My energetic frequency had raised to the point of disconnecting with the physical world. I no longer saw the hospital or the staff and I no longer saw my physical body.

I have heard that some people who have a Near Death Experience (NDE) event have a sensation of moving through a tunnel as well as a life review. I did not have either of those experiences. I went directly from the bird's-eye view of my body to the light.

I realized I was a sparkling orb of intelligent energy floating in eternity. I had no feelings of regret, stress, or anger or any other negative emotion. I was truly a Be-ing; full of wholeness and completeness. There were no feelings of lack or wanting.

I was then drawn closer to a beautiful white-gold light. The sound! Every time I try to describe the sounds, the memory of those frequencies brings me to tears. Like music but with vibrations so beautiful, so pure and so etheric they were beyond description. I was vibrating at the frequency and the sound of God.

Then I merged with the light. I was being swallowed up by a knowledge that was greater than all of humanity. I was becoming One with God. There was no place that I stopped and God started, we were One. A truly blissful feeling came over me, like honey being poured into every atom of my being. I felt no fear, no stress, no anxiety, no anger, no resentments. Re-birthed into an existence that had never known ego, or anything physical or material, or anything negative; this was my new state of being-ness. Pure unconditional love. That is truly what it means to be God. I was experiencing God. I WAS GOD! The bliss was amazing. In fact it was indescribable. As

I savored the blissful experience, there was an exchange or a download of information that took place from God to me. And there was a bestowing of special gifts that I will reveal later.

I heard, felt and knew that there was no separation between me and God. I had no regret about dying. I had come home. I was feeling more complete than I had ever remembered. I was experiencing the One-ness of the All. I now had the knowing of total truth, total love, total beauty. I left the fragmented world of the physical and entered the completeness of God. I was whole. I was truly a Be-ing. The pure love of God and I had no beginning and no ending. We were one unit. One energy I had shed my human-ness and was experiencing the release of anything that was not perfect. I savored the ecstasy of being One with God Consciousness for what felt like hours.

Then, I felt a tug on my heart. My daughter, just thirteen at the time, called to me. Although she would later let me know that she had no idea her spirit had requested my return, I knew I had to go back into my physical body and finish raising her. It took every ounce or wave of will that I could pull together to "plead my case" with God. Jennifer was my only daughter from a previous marriage. I knew in every increment of my spirit body that I needed to leave this perfect paradise and return to my physical shell and the 3-D world that waited below me.

I was allowed to go back to my body, a process that was cumbersome and heavy and uncomfortable. As I re-entered my physical body I felt the weight and all the restrictions that were connected to it. I had been totally absorbed by God for only three minutes – a life-changing three minutes. It all happened very quickly but in my heart it left a timeless mark that would propel me on a quest for the rest of this lifetime. This one three-minute event expanded beyond all time and space for me. It opened doors and changed my spiritual choices and life path forever.

As I later reflected on the event I realized there were specific lessons that I will share with you here, that were downloaded into my opalescent, energetic orb when I merged with God. First, I learned that time moves very differently in the spirit world. It felt like I had been dead for many hours or even days but in reality it was only about three minutes. This concept of time was reinforced for me later, during other experiences in the astral planes.

Secondly, I realized I had been suspended approximately one mile above my physical body as I looked down on it right before I merged with God. For many years I reflected on the vision of looking down on a one-inch-long body and I wondered how far up my spirit had been to have that perspective. So one day I drove out to a flat, straight road in Eastern Colorado and found a stop sign that was approximately the same height as me, 5'4. Then I drove away from it and kept watch in the rear view mirror until it looked approximately one inch long and measured the distance between me and the sign: One mile!

Another lesson I learned from this experience is that when you are out of your body you can see through walls, ceilings, floors and any other obstacle. This was helpful to me later on as a Remote Viewer.

The concept that our thoughts, feelings and memories remain with our spirit bodies was also reinforced through my Near Death Experience. I had previously had that perception when my spirit body spontaneously popped out of my physical body many years before. This supported the concept that our physical bodies are meaningless and insignificant.

Returning to my physical body as a changed person, I realized God's plan for me was to teach others about death and dying.

It is now estimated that 5 percent of the population of the United States has had a Near Death Experience. As medical science progresses and more and more people are brought back into their bodies after a traumatic experience, we will see the planet continue to evolve spiritually. Is it possible that your doctor could have agreed prior to this lifetime to facilitate your spiritual evolution?

Three
Life's Purpose Unfolding

"What happens when you take a million ordinary citizens and turn them into extraordinary psychics? Evolution!"
"Extraordinary Psychic" by Debra Katz.

Prior to my Near Death Experience (NDE), my life consisted of living weekend to weekend. I spent my days planning Super Bowl parties, living in an upscale neighborhood, and working out. at the club to sculpt my beyond-fit body. My life was so materially and physically focused that I even planned a party to welcome our new Volvo into our home, inviting all of our friends to attend and see our new status symbol. I was married to "The Trust Fund Kid". He had grown up in a family of great material wealth and our lives were based on the accumulation of material things and drinking alcohol. Our primary focus was on having a good time.

After my NDE, my life went through dramatic changes. I stopped being the party girl, I stopped taking drugs, prescription and recreational. I exchanged my friends for ones who were more spiritually evolved. I could no longer be in the presence of negativity. I stopped watching the news. I stopped associating with any negative people. My perception of how to live my life shifted from being focused on myself to one of serving others. I began taking classes to develop my healing abilities that had made themselves evident to me many years before, when I spontaneously healed my young daughter of her headaches.

I realized that it was time for me to discontinue my search through many religious organizations to find the "right spiritual path." I now truly understood what God was. I had a knowing of God and an acute awareness that It was inside me. My spirit had re- united with God even though it had been for just a brief few minutes. I had been God. I was now an instrument of His or Hers or Theirs. For me God was no longer defined in human terms but as energy; powerful, life-affirming energy; the energy of the Creator.

I spent the next decade and more attending many healing classes to develop and enhance my God-given talents and to uncover my Divine life's purpose. A glimmer of those abilities were revealed to me in 1975 when my daughter was four years old. She had been attacked frequently by severe pain in her head. Many doctor appointments and medical tests had not provided a diagnosis.

We were at a shopping mall in a bookstore when one of the attacks came on. She started screaming in pain. As an empathic mother who is connected energetically to her child, I felt her pain. I felt it intensely. My daughter and I had always been deeply connected. I came close to passing out when she had to have a vaccination at the doctor's office. So now, this extreme headache attack, while in the chaotic energy of the shopping mall, was debilitating to both of us. This happened many years prior to my NDE. I did not feel connected to God at that time but I was grasping for help as if my fingernails were clenched to the edge of a cliff. I panicked and asked for an answer, any answer from anywhere. And then it came to me. A voice in my head said, *"Put your hands on her and we will take the pain away."* Desperate for any solution, I did not question where this message came from. I took her out to the common area of the mall, sat on a bench and laid her head in my lap with her body stretched across the bench. I placed my hands on her head just as I had been instructed by 'who knows who.' I felt I was not in control of what was happening, I was just the instrument of a force that was taking over my body. A strange calmness came over me as if I had been wrapped in a warm blanket. Within a few short minutes the pain was gone. I was vastly relieved and also quite astonished. I had been receiving messages in my head since I was sixteen but this was the first time I had specific instruction on how to be a healer.

I later realized that my daughter had become a facilitator of my learning. She was my teacher, helping me to embrace the role of healer that would evolve later to much higher levels. I was then driven to attend every healing class that I could find; Tibetan healing, Lakota Indian healing, aromatherapy, crystal healing, Reiki. A force greater than myself presented many alternative healing classes to me as preparation to heal others with God working though my hands. I began healing clients nights and weekends while living the life of an insurance agent forty hours per week.

Almost twenty years since my Near Death Experience, I still had not forgotten The Bliss and I was deep into a quest to experience The Bliss again. I needed Oneness with God. I craved it. Nothing in the mundane world made any sense to me anymore. The physical world seemed petty, contrived and without substance. For many years I had followed my quest. I felt I no longer had anything in common with my friends. My entire world was shifting. I went through a divorce, changed careers, changed friends, changed the way I dressed and what I talked about. I changed everything that had been important to me. The old ragged rug had been pulled out from under my life and replaced with a new magic carpet. I saw possibilities where they had not existed before. Some of the changes were consciously initiated by me. I know some of them were chosen by God. Looking back on it now, I understand that all of it was God's plan; She just let me think I was making some of the decisions. I was being guided and groomed for a path that lay before me and I had no idea I would meet a teacher who would be my twin flame and accelerate the execution of my life's purpose.

If you look back on the experiences of your life, you may realize that God has been grooming you for great things – to work on His team and to touch many lives in a positive way. Many times we get caught up in our busy lives reading emails and connecting on Facebook, and we forget that there is most likely a higher purpose to our lives.

As I looked back on all of the extraordinary events – the spontaneous out-of-body experiences, the messages that came to me through the radio, my NDE, the guidance to be a healer, the advice to take a class in Remote Viewing, meeting Michael – all of those puzzle pieces came together and groomed me for great things. Knowing and living my life's purpose continues to be my only reason to remain in this body.

Four
The Quest for Bliss

"Once more I found myself out of my body,
possessed of a freedom which I could never describe."
"The Projection of the Astral Body"
by Sylvan Muldoon and Hereward Carrington.

Following my bliss-filled Near Death Experience, I found that living in the 3-D world was frustrating and at times unbearable. I longed to have "vacations" to the other side where I could recharge and regroup to get back on center. I started reading everything I could get my hands on about Near Death and Out-of-Body experiences. Mostly I found books on astral travel which appeared to be a way to leave my physical body behind in hopes of reconnecting deeply with God. I began doing exercises I found in a book called the "Astral Projection Workbook" by J.H. Brennan. I would take one or more weekends per month and go to our cabin in the Colorado mountains where there was no phone, no computer, no T.V. and no other 3-D world distractions.

I had some success with the Astral Projection Workbook. Entering into a deep, deep meditation I followed the exercises in the book. The book instructed readers to practice immediately after waking up. This is because of the altered brain wave state that we experience during sleep. The brain wave state is called hypnagogic; being on the edge between wakefulness and sleep. I would faithfully practice my travels as soon as I woke up. I could feel my spirit leaving my body and I would begin by just projecting my spirit to another part of the room, sit in the chair and look at my physical body as the observer. I felt quite at home doing this since I had experienced out-of-body sensations previously. I was quite happy with my progress, however, I was not having the experience I was looking for. I wanted to merge with God again and feel the complete bliss that I had known within my Near Death Experience.

Next I projected my spirit body outside the cabin. This felt more unsettling as I was no longer looking at my physical body but of course I knew that my silver cord was attached and that I would be able to find my way back. I felt free from my physical body. I was full of wonderment and excitement of what the adventure would hold for me. Rising up about fifty feet in the air, I looked down on the roof of the cabin and the surrounding pine trees and I noticed one small yellow dandelion blooming near the porch. I practiced zooming my vision in and out, moving my spirit body closer and farther from an object. I viewed the dandelion up close. Then I zoomed in on a pinecone, a quartzite rock and a few other things. I floated over the dirt road in front of the cabin and took a look at the creek that flowed next to it. I started to feel a little uneasy and decided it was time to return to my physical shell that lay on the Murphy bed in the old cabin. I set my intention to return and magically my spirit passed through the ceiling and walls and re-entered my physical body. I was relieved that my intention was followed without any force or major determination. I just thought about where I wanted my spirit to go and it went there.

I thought I had done an excellent job of my first "self- directed" astral projection outside the cabin. However, when I stood up I felt dizzy. I tried to walk into the kitchen area and I ran into the side of the doorway. I felt disjointed and not really connected to my physical body. I was not certain how to correct this issue. It was as if my spirit body was overlapping my physical body by about a foot. I also felt mentally rattled and unfocused. And then I realized that I had not been able to project to higher frequency dimensions. I needed a teacher.

I continued to work with the workbook while looking for a teacher. I tested myself by astral traveling outside of the cabin, making note of something that I saw; a blossom, a rock, a feather lying on the ground. Then after returning to my body I would walk outside to get confirmation.

The more I experimented, the more I realized that we all have this ability. We were spirit bodies first and we will be spirit bodies last. We all have the ability to leave the confinement of our physical bodies and experience the extraordinary life beyond.

As I built on my successes I felt I was definitely developing a skill to astral travel but I was not accomplishing two things that were important to me. I was not experiencing any of The Bliss and I was not integrating back into my physical body successfully. The need for a teacher became a priority. I was later taught that I was not traveling to astral realms that were of very high frequency to experience God. There are many layers of differing frequencies within the astral planes and my spirit traveling outside of the cabin was not connecting me to Oneness.

My integration back into my body was awkward and I was not certain how to correct this issue. The lack of correct integration into my physical body left me off kilter and uncoordinated. I was concerned about driving a car or doing other mundane activities safely.

I knew I needed a teacher that could help me go to the next level. I shared my quest with a metaphysical friend of mine who suggested a class in Remote Viewing which he thought was similar.

Remote Viewing as I understood it at that time was a military-oriented type of astral travel and the chance of the training taking me to higher frequencies to be near God was slim but at least I could learn to reintegrate my spiritual body with my physical body correctly. I had no other choices at that time so I decided to sign up for the

Remote Viewing class, hoping the instructor would be able to help me progress to the next level with my quest. Little did I know that the decision to take the class was all Divinely orchestrated.

Five
Holographic Slideshow

*"Since all time is an omnipresent 'now,' it can be accessed
by us at any point if we find a way to break free of
the constraints of physical thinking."*
"Astral Projection for Beginners."
by Edain McCoy.

I knew he was going to make me late. He hated that I had anything that would be my own, anything that excluded him. Breaking eye contact, I kept moving toward the door. I had to make it to the Remote Viewing class. I felt as if my life depended on it. Now, no matter what, I was going to be late. What if they would already be in trance and not let me in? Cutting off the chit-chat, I darted out the door and quickly accomplished the twenty-minute drive to Wings Metaphysical Bookstore in Wheat Ridge, Colorado.

I scurried to the classroom at the back of the store. The door was closed and the class was in progress. Gingerly, I pushed the door open. Peering in, I saw the instructor, Michael Van Atta, standing with his back to me, facing a semicircle of about twenty students. He turned around to look at me and at that moment our entire lives changed. Michael and I locked gazes. Before us like a holographic slide show, images of our lifetimes together were projected in the space between us. Lifetimes as teachers and students, as monks, as brothers, as parent and child, and many, many other roles that we had played as we came together over and over again in a multitude of lifetimes. It quickly became apparent that this was the real reason I had been Divinely guided to take this class. The intense motivation to attend the class was not just about learning Remote Viewing or how to integrate my spirit back into my body correctly.

Michael, a student of David Morehouse, had a teaching style that was filled with humor. It was so joyful for my heart to be near him. Although he was teaching Remote Viewing, which is a military application of astral travel, he did not focus on the rigid military protocols. He focused on the spiritual connection that we feel when we leave our bodies. He was speaking my language!

Many times our viewings would be to connect with Jesus of Nazareth, or to view the energy involved with the levitations of St. Joseph of Cupertino. For me, a non-military oriented student, these viewings were intriguing.

I sat down at that first class in the front row full of anticipation. Michael was funny and animated and I felt so connected to him. He placed a wooden box in front of us, told us to send our consciousness into the box, access information and then return to draw pictures and list aspects of the target. I was a little nervous about stacking up to the others in the group, not knowing what their experience or training entailed, but Michael acted as if this took no special talent. It was something we should all be able to accomplish. That helped me go boldly into the box.

I did my best and drew a four sided cross that had equidistant legs, like a Celtic cross, and then felt that there were "flaps" of something along each leg, like layers. I did my best to draw them. I picked up the energy of yellow and red; vibrant colors; and I felt the texture of cloth. The center of the cross felt empty to me almost as if the rest of the item had an energy but the center did not.

Michael went around the room and asked a few of the students what aspects they got. I was very uneasy when he called on me as my information did not match the others. I went ahead and shared what I got, deciding that I had to put my ego in my pocket and not worry about being right. I also showed him the picture I had drawn.

With a big smile, Michael produced the target for all of us to see. It was a New Mexico flag, yellow and red with the Zia on it, the Pueblo symbol of life depicting the sun in the center of a four-sided cross. My impressions were considered excellent for a beginner and I was immediately hooked.

Next he placed another box on the table, this time a metal box and my mind immediately thought, *"This is going to be more difficult because the metal will keep me from getting clear information."* However, I did my best and I drew a picture of a cantilevered object, got the energy of the color blue, and the energy of plastic as well as metal. I could see there was some sort of symbol on the blue part but was not sure what it was.

With apprehension I waited for Michael to open the box. When he opened it, I knew I was totally hooked! It was a Russian switchblade with a blue plastic handle and a painting of a woman on the handle. I was getting much needed positive reinforcement from this class.

Learning to Remote View using items in boxes is something that you can practice at home. Since this is something that everyone is capable of doing, it is a matter of removing the negative self-talk and allowing yourself to embrace this Divinely-gifted skill.

After class I approached Michael and discussed the issue I was having integrating my spirit body into my physical body upon re-entry from astral travel. Michael counseled me to go home, lie down and expand my spirit body to a larger space and then let it "shrink wrap" back to my physical body shape. I visualized this process as similar to expanding a rubber band and then letting it snap back into its correct shape. I went home and tried it and it worked perfectly for me. I was elated to have found a competent teacher who did not judge my strange questions but validated them and my abilities.

Often I stayed after the weekly class to talk with Michael and ask him all of the questions I had waited patiently for an answer.

Michael addressed the issue of bliss by sending all of the class to the Holy of Holies, the most sacred place where God resides, to Remote View the energy there. Many of us returned from that viewing with tears in our eyes due to the intensely blissful experience. I learned that to experience bliss at will, which was one of my priorities, I needed to be traveling to very high-frequency realms. My travels that were fifty feet above my mountain cabin were not going to give me that experience.

Taking the class from Michael was quenching a thirst that had plagued me for a very long time. And as an important added bonus, I connected to my twin flame! Throughout the class Michael and I continued to lock eyes. There was so much going on energetically and I just couldn't wait to come back each week for another class.

The class met every Wednesday night and during the week we had homework. Homework consisted of sending our consciousness to the boxes located at Michael's home in Arvada, Colorado and accessing information. I quickly became proficient with Remote Viewing, possibly because I had helpers on the other side who had been with me for many, many years. Also I knew that my NDE had opened me up psychically. I will share more information about my spirit helpers later on.

Michael would intersperse the viewings with some history of Remote Viewing as well as targets that were spiritual or what he called "off earth," such as viewing the dark side of the moon or the healing energy of the water at Lourdes. It was common in his classes for us to leave our bodies and visit the Egyptian pyramids or the energy of a cancer cell changing back to a healthy cell. Certainly this was not a Remote Viewing class that was totally structured or focused on military protocols and it was just what I needed.

Meeting in this lifetime was no chance encounter. We were two divinely connected spirits who were meant to do God's work together. This was a pivotal moment in our lives and over the twelve years that followed, we would become each other's teachers again, just as we had experienced in other lifetimes. Michael taught me so much about astral travel and Remote Viewing and I taught him about using crystals and essential oils for healing and introduced him to Reiki.

We would go on to accomplish profound healings together, produce successful Remote Viewings, astral travel and accomplish many other spiritual acts that would be the product of us reconnecting. In fact working murder cases together was probably the most important interaction that established a deep connection between us. I will share more about that later on in this book.

Six
Etheric Helpers

"I am certain from firsthand experience that God figures, saints, and yogis such as Jesus, Mary, Buddha, and Paramahansa Yogananda continue to exist in spirit form. (Fortunately they don't care what religion you are!) They will often spontaneously appear to clairvoyants, healers, and even laypeople when their type of energy is needed and welcomed."
"Extraordinary Psychic" by Debra Katz.

"I believe in God, but not as one thing, not as an old man in the sky. I believe that what people call God is something in all of us. I believe that what Jesus and Mohammed and Buddha and all the rest said was right. It's just that the translations have gone wrong."
John Lennon

Many of us are aware that we have spirit guides around us, helping us through life. You may remember times in your life when you were aware that someone was watching over you. This awareness is one of the ways you can take your relationship with them to the next level. Over time guides can come and go. I have had some guides who have been with me from the beginning of this life and I think they may stay for the duration.

When I first met Michael, I knew I had worked with guides but I knew nothing about them. I could feel their presence around me especially during healing sessions with clients. Even back when I was twenty-five and my daughter had the headache issue, I knew there was someone or something that had orchestrated the healing. I had only been a vehicle to help that healing take place. Before that, as I began to receive messages from the other side as a teenager and during some very special experiences in my life, I felt that I had helpers or guides that were around me in spirit. Their presence originally became clear to me when I heard my deceased grandmother speaking to me through the radio when I was about sixteen. I never realized I could actually develop a relationship with these powerful entities. This was another important piece of information that would fill gaps in my spiritual quest. I knew I had guides around me, helping me and giving me messages from God, but I did not know their names or why they had chosen me to work with. I had not taken the time to get to know them.

Michael suggested that I go into trance and call in each spirit guide one at a time and ask their names, find out what their expertise is and why were they with me. One of the guides, Shadow Man, also called Bardo, came forward to assist me with my life's work helping others to connect with deceased loved ones. With his help I eventually went on to teach many workshops in this subject.

Connecting with spirit guides in this way has been a beneficial exercise and I was able to have a much better working relationship with them after I did that. Still, guides do come and go.

One day shortly after moving to Sedona, Arizona while I was working with a client to help her restore her hearing, John Lennon came in as a guide for the first time. I was amazed. I was thinking of him as a rock star. I was not thinking of what an evolved being he is. After the healing session ended, I reflected on why he had shown up and then I realized that he is an ascended being; a true master. He changed the world with his work. John Lennon dedicated his life to touching the lives of millions, helping them to achieve a higher level of consciousness. I feel very fortunate to have John Lennon as one of my guides.

Dream November, 2014
Four Months After Michael Passed Away
"I am here to help you resonate with a guide that represents the other side without seeming too old or different." Lennon smiles and then calls Michael forward from the shadows.

I am very surprised to find Michael and John Lennon together.

Michael (in spirit) grins and says *"Yeah, I have been hanging out with this guy."*

I am in awe. *"Do you have any idea who this is?"* I know that Michael missed the entire Beatles era while he was in Vietnam and he has no idea how important I think Lennon is.

Michael says, *"Yes, he is a very evolved being."*

"He is one of the Beatles!" I say with great energetic potency pushing my voice through restricted vocal cords and out of my mouth..

Lennon pipes up and says, *"None of that Beatles stuff matters up here, sweetheart!"*

Michael grins and says, *"Well, anyway, that is not what he is known for around here! He is here to help people of this lifetime evolve and open their hearts and to change their thinking!"*

I feel a strong shift of energy flowing from my heart to Michael's. We enjoy the energy exchange for many minutes. There is so much love between us.

Then Michael says, *"I know it is hard for you to remain when I am on this side but I am here for you always, every day, 24/7."*

John Lennon opened my eyes to the fact that my talents had been developed to help others evolve spiritually; not on the immense scale that he did, but in my own way through this book as well as through workshops that I teach and helping one client at a time to heal spiritually.

Another guide that was a surprise to me was Jesus because he came to me at a time I felt at odds with the Christian faith. My perception of Jesus was within the sacrificial concept and imposed rules. Not what I would have considered spiritual.

I did not think of Jesus as a healer until he appeared one day in the middle of a healing session. He entered the room during a session that I was doing in Colorado on a client who had been diagnosed with multiple sclerosis. During the healing I felt his presence but I questioned it. *"Jesus, is that really you?"*

"Yes my child, I know you are at odds with the Christian faith and what that means in the modern world, but I come to you as the Supreme Healer. That is what I know and that is what I do. My healing powers are available to all who want them."

I meditated on this experience. Jesus gave me a better perspective on the contortions that the Christian faith has gone through since the time he actually walked on the earth. I learned not to hold onto my frustrations against him that involved the twisting of his original concepts. I integrated Jesus's healing energy into my healing practice and I know he is there with me as I meet with my clients. My relationship with Jesus helped me to build confidence in my healing abilities and has given me renewed acceptance of the original concepts of Christian faith.

In 2011 I had an aura photograph done by Jamie at Center for the New Age in Sedona, Arizona. A large spirit guide appeared in this photo standing in back of me, his arms outstretched. Jamie was amazed, stating that she had never seen such a large and powerful spirit guide show up on an aura photo before. Many people who have seen this photo have stated that Jesus is standing over me, watching over me and showing up in my aura.

I have many other guides that come to help me within my psychic and healing work. I feel I have this connection due to my NDE as well as other out-of-body experiences that have built and strengthened the connection to the other side of the veil.

I feel deepest gratitude to Michael for teaching me to connect to my guides on a deeper level. It has really boosted my abilities as they work through me.

If you are working with guides and have not taken the opportunity to get to know them, try calling them in one by one. This is a valuable exercise to strengthen your relationship with them.

Seven

Michael Scouts Out the Landscape

"...consciousness is what gives the brain life - it is the invisible life essence that animates the brain. It is the unseen aspect of self, both aware and unaware, both conscious and subconscious, using the brain to capture thoughts, and then coalescing them to create the mind."
"Evolve Your Brain" by Joe Dispenza. D.C.

Michael and I both brought the knowledge of the astral planes to our relationship as a result of our individual out-of-body experiences. Michael met with God while in a coma. Being in a coma is similar to dying. The silver cord is still attached but only tentatively. A person in a coma is not in their body during that time and is experiencing altered brain wave activity.

When he was just five years old, Michael had a severe head injury that put him in the hospital in a coma for about six weeks. Michael's injury caused brain damage, making it necessary for him to relearn how to walk and talk again. This event also opened Michael psychically. I now understand this event was God grooming him for our later work together as alternative healers and Remote Viewers.

While in the coma, Michael had his version of a NDE. He said he remembered going to a room like a classroom and sitting in a chair toward the back of the room. There was a luminous being standing at the front of the room and he was talking but Michael could not hear what he was saying. The other children were sitting up closer to the front of the room and after what Michael thought was twenty minutes, the luminous being came to him and said "It's your time to go back." What he thought was twenty minutes was actually six weeks.

After this experience, Michael developed psychic abilities that helped him to avoid traffic accidents, survive some close calls in Vietnam and to facilitate miraculous healings.

Six weeks in the physical world equaled twenty minutes in the astral planes while in a coma. This was confirmation for me that time moves differently in the astral planes. Michael and I had both experienced it. As we later used astral travel to do remote healings, Remote Viewings or effecting matter remotely we realized that a great amount of work could be accomplished in such a short time in the astral planes. Time can slow down or speed up.

Michael made a remarkable recovery in having to learn to walk and talk all over again at age five. God had a plan for him. Michael would go on to accomplish many healings and to assist many others in their transition to the spirit world.

As I look back on how Michael and I met, how God groomed each of us separately to do his work and how we were brought together, I am in awe. I saw the entire plan like a well-orchestrated opera flash in my vision. Michael and I had both met with God; Michael as a child, me as an adult. These experiences gave us both a comfort level with death that groomed us to fulfill our life's purpose of helping others evolve spiritually. We would go on to help others transition to the other side in a deathing process. I understood that our entire lives brought us to this focus as part of the divine plan to do God's work; to help others to connect to and develop their spiritual lives and to move into One-ness. We would go forward together to make the planet a better place, one person at a time.

Later on, in 2010, Michael and I were both interviewed by Josie Varga for her book "Visits to Heaven," documenting our out-of-body experiences.

Eight
Who Needs Dr. Kevorkian?

"She made the decision that her existence had lost its meaning. And you cannot judge that."
Dr. Jack Kevorkian

What better gift could a Dad give his daughter than the ability to leave a cancer-infested body, to help her transition to the other side of the veil and experience Oneness? Michael had studied Robert Monroe's system of helping people go to Transition Park. He had used that system to help many people cross over to the other side, including his mother.

Transition Park is an astral location where spirits getting ready to cross over can be greeted by their deceased loved ones before the silver cord breaks for the permanent shift of consciousness. Robert Monroe was a pioneer in astral projection or out-of-body experiences; in fact, he originally coined the term Out of Body Experience and created the Monroe Institute, which trains people to astral project and learn Remote Viewing. Robert Monroe also came up with the term "Transition Park."

This is a process that Michael and I incorporated into our sessions many times to help release fear for those ready to transition. We also accomplished many soul rescues in which a disincarnate spirit was brought to Transition Park and met with loved ones to complete their process. Sometimes when souls are forced out of the physical body in a traumatic way, they are confused and earth-bound and need some assistance to cross over. This was a way of putting the person at ease, a way of showing them the landscape.

Michael's daughter Megan was diagnosed with breast cancer at age twenty-eight. It was a tragic diagnosis for a young woman. Megan went through traditional treatments, including surgery, chemotherapy and radiation but over the next five years, cancer took over and settled in her brain with multiple tumors.

Knowing that Megan was reaching the end of her life, we had recently visited her in Pennsylvania. Michael spent much quality time with her in discussions about the astral planes.

A few days after we returned home we got a call from Michael's older daughter, Erin. "Dad," Erin said from the other side of the phone call, "Megan is ready to transition but she is afraid." Michael hung up the phone and informed me of Erin's call. We immediately sat in our side-by-side lounge chairs, feet up, and went into trance in tandem to help her. In this case, we were to accomplish helping a spirit that was ready to leave the body and make the transition – much like I helped Michael make his transition years later.

Within any type of energetic healing, even the kind where there is a clearly spoken request for help, it is important to ask permission to proceed. This is done by the healer sending their consciousness or spirit body to the spirit of the person they are healing to ask permission. In this case the healing would be assisting Megan to leave her body. The answer to this request does not always agree with what was discussed in a preliminary verbal conversation. As Michael and I sat in our chairs in Colorado and entered trance, we sent our spirit bodies to meet with Megan's spirit body in Pennsylvania. I approached Megan about permission. She let me know that she did not want me to help. This was something that was just between Megan and her Dad and although I was disappointed, I honored that request. I held the energy of the space by just sending the heartfelt intent of love to the situation while Michael went to work.

About fifteen minutes later, we both emerged from trance and shared our experiences. This was typical of our remote sessions. I shared with Michael that Megan wanted to keep this very intimate process between her and him and that I had honored the request.

Michael, with tears in his eyes, shared with me that he took Megan's spirit to Transition Park as he had done so many times with clients who were ready to cross over. Their two spirits sat on the bench, waiting for relatives and friends who had crossed over to greet her. Megan was greeted by many glowing and loving luminous spirits, including her grandmother. Michael then told Megan, *"Megan, when you are ready, this is where you will go."*

Megan's reply to Michael was unwavering. *"I am ready now, Dad,"* she said.

Michael left Megan's spirit in Transition Park with her deceased loved ones and returned to his body.

As we sat in our chairs and discussed our experiences, the sound of the phone ringing pierced our foggy re-entry discussion. It was Erin crying tears of relief. *"She's gone, Dad. Thank you so much for helping her. She's no longer in pain!"*

Now the tears flowed freely. Michael and I sat wrapped in each other's arms and cried tears of grief, tears of relief and tears of gratitude.

The energy of grief can be heavy and burdensome. It is an energy of closure and regret and the deep sadness that pulls on your heart. Grief for a parent losing a child can be the most unnerving emotional pain ever. However, when spending so much time in the astral planes and knowing what a blissful experience it is to become One with God, there is no greater gift than helping a child cross over into death when she is ready. Few fathers will ever have such an intimate and important experience with their children.

Our society seems to think that death is the worst thing that could happen to a person and so they do everything humanly possible to keep someone alive even during extreme and painful conditions. If you have a loved one who is ready to make the transition, it is very helpful if you release them and bless the process. Let go of the emotional hold you have over them, give them permission and allow them to go into the Bliss. This is a wonderful parting gift that you have the ability to give.

Nine

This Little Piggy Came From Heaven

"A strong spirit transcends rules."
Jesse Jackson

Long before my mother passed away, I wrote her a letter describing my Near Death Experience. My mother always had an intense fear of death. It was common for families to lose one or two children back then and my mother's baby sister had passed away after just one month of being in her physical body. My grandmother, for some strange and unknown reason, made my mother, as a little child, touch the dead baby. This dreadful experience imprinted a dark cloud over my mother. As her years passed, and she entered her eighties, of course, death began to loom over her thoughts. I wanted to help her with my unique knowledge of my blissful experience. I wrote the letter and mailed it to her and she was quite surprised, as I had never shared the information with her at the time it happened more than twenty years earlier. After she died I found that she had saved my letter in one of her photo albums, showing me that it had been important to her.

Both of my parents were cremated and their ashes scattered along the Arizona Trail near the small town of Oracle, Arizona where they lived. It is a beautiful desert location with a magical feeling of twilight energy; many native plants seem to glow and reach out to you. On the final day of emptying their home to ready it for sale, I stopped by the trail where their ashes were scattered to have a little chat with them. I walked out on the trail and took a few pictures hoping to pick up orbs of Mom and Dad's energy signatures. As I called in their spirits for communication, I snapped some pictures with my digital camera.

I stood there and I asked my Mother for confirmation regarding my NDE. "Mom, how is it there on the other side? I shared with you many years ago the blissful experience I had when I died and met with God. Tell me, is that what you are experiencing? Are you filled with bliss? If so, can you give me a sign to let me know that you are One with God?" I was not sure what kind of response I would get as my Mother had not been a deeply spiritual person. In my head, I heard my Mother's voice. *"What kind of a sign? What can I do that will give you confirmation in a form that you will recognize?"*

I answered, *"Well, Mom, how about this? When I leave here, make something cross the road in front of my car that makes me say 'Oh my gosh!', okay?"*

Silence.... I did not hear any response. *"Okay,"* I said to myself, *"If I am to get an answer, one will come."* I got in the car and drove on. Nothing. Fifteen minutes went by, nothing.

Twenty minutes later, I was driving out of Oracle and heading toward the Phoenix airport. I had the radio on and I was singing along to the Rolling Stones song *"Can't You Hear Me Knocking."* I laughed at the irony of the timing of that song. At first feeling hopeful that it was my Mother's way of answering me, however it did not fit the specific request.

All of a sudden appearing from nowhere, a mother and baby javelina stood in the middle of the road staring at me. I slammed on my brakes to avoid hitting them. They did not move. They just stood there looking other-worldly with direct eye contact. Out of my mouth popped *"Oh my gosh!"* and then, realizing what I said and what it meant, once again the words popped out of my mouth *"OH MY GOSH!!!"* I had received a true, priceless gift from the other side, compliments of my Mother. I felt deep gratitude for this coming together of events that gave me confirmation.

Javelina are similar to wild pigs or boars but are actually Peccaries. They are typically nocturnal. It is rare to see one at 11:00 in the morning and especially a mom and a baby standing in the middle of the street not moving and both offering direct eye contact. This was clearly a message from my mother. And so now I knew that my mother was experiencing the bliss that I had also experienced so many years ago during a surgery gone wrong that some might have thought was an accident. I think it was divinely inspired. I sat in the car looking at the javelina and sobbed. What a special gift from my Mother to send these animals to me.

Javelina as animal totems are considered to be shape shifters. How appropriate for my Mother to manifest this signal for me from the other side. This divine message of confirmation that my Mother was in Bliss is a priceless gift to me from heaven.

Later on I examined the photos I took out there on the Arizona Trail. At the base of some of the photos is a very special energy that is pyramid shaped, glowing with a pale blue light that has tiny white lights around its perimeter, and is surrounded by a magenta-colored shadow. More confirmation that my parents were with me on that very special day. Thank you, Mom and Dad!

If you sense that a deceased loved one is around you, you could take some photographs and look for orbs or other evidence of energies around you. This is a way of confirming what you are feeling and will help you to develop your talents in sensing those energies.

Ten
God's Secret Language

"Vibrations, which constitute everything in the known cosmos, from sub- atomic particles to galaxies, compose the Living Spirit. Everything we know or can conceive is connected within these vibrations. Readers will come to recognize the Living Spirit within themselves and will learn to step beyond their physical limitations. Whoever reaches an understanding or comparable teachings will assist the evolution of earth during the present cataclysmic period."
"Under the Plum Tree, The Tao of Everything" Chung Fu.

God speaks to us in many ways. If we are listening, we can hear the messages. Usually that means being still enough to screen out life's distractions. Taking time to meditate and center in is an important part of that process. The military taught their Remote Viewers to go into long periods of mediation prior to accomplishing their viewings. After many years of Remote Viewing and astral traveling, Michael and I were able to achieve an altered brain state within minutes and leave our physical bodies behind. Once out of body, we could tap into the energy signature of a target.

One way God speaks to us is through an energy exchange. Everything contains energy. There is a secret language within energy frequencies that offers Remote Viewers and astral travelers a wealth of information. As living beings we have energy within us and around us. We can feel it if we ground static electricity after walking across carpet. This is one confirmation that we are energetic beings. Acknowledging that the lifeless body of a deceased person has lost their energetic spirit within the deathing process is another way to keenly tap into the fact that we are energetic beings. When I had my Near Death Experience one very important piece of information was the knowing that all of who I am, through many lifetimes, is contained in my spirit or energetic body. The physical body held no emotion, memories or intellect. Thinking of yourself as an energetic being is very important to be effective in accomplishing etheric work.

God sends messages to us through an energy exchange. When we are in a life-threatening situation without any words being spoken, our spirit body sends signals to our physical body that triggers a chemical change of flight or fight response. The chemical change is first triggered by information that is exchanged energetically. If someone is coming up behind you to attack you, you do not need to turn around and see them to recognize this trigger. Your energetic body can pick up the need for fear and this is God messaging you to respond for survival.

There is knowledge exchanged between human energy fields all of the time. Remember a time when you were near a person who made you feel drained of energy? Someone you might call an energy vampire? Or someone who made you feel uplifted or spiritual by just being in their presence such as the Dalai Lama? Learning to identify soul signatures is an important part of astral travel as well as Remote Viewing.

Something that you can practice is an awareness of energy exchange when you are near someone. When your dog walks into the room, do you feel a shift of the vibration? Does your dog's energy change when he or she moves near you? This is an awareness that can be applied in many areas of your life, such as business interactions or holiday dinners with relatives.

In the 1960's Grover Cleveland (Cleve) Backster performed experiments using a lie detector to communicate with plants. Backster was an interrogation specialist for the CIA. The machine is typically used to measure the change of the galvanic skin response as well as a subtle change in the pace of breath. These physiological changes can be an indication of a person telling the truth or a lie. Because telling a lie is incongruent with the natural energy of your spirit, it triggers a physical response that the machine can measure. Backster connected the machine to his houseplants and noted a reaction when he communicated with them. He found that it would take only a thought about hurting a plant and the plant would react. So he did not have to actually physically harm the plant, only just transmit the thought of harm, for the plant to have a reaction that was recorded by the lie detector. Backster also found that he could transmit the thoughts from a distance, even from another state across the country and he was able to record a reaction from the plant. This is evidence that we can connect and communicate with the energy signature of a person or thing located a long way from us. These experiments were documented in a book called "The Secret Life of Plants" by Peter Tompkins and Christopher Bird.

Acknowledging that everything has a spirit with a soul signature, Michael and I were able to leave our physical bodies and have experiences that we would not have had otherwise. When we first met that night in Remote Viewing class, it was our soul signatures that recognized each other from past lifetimes. The soul signature does not dramatically change from one lifetime to another. There are subtle changes that take place due to a lifetime of experiences but for the most part, the soul signature remains recognizable from one lifetime to the next.

Humans are not the only banks of energetic information. Walls, ceilings, rocks, dirt, plants, furniture, automobiles, homes and all other things store energy. Some materials store energy better than others. Quartz crystals for instance are known to be programmable. When events happen near rocks that have quartz crystals the energy of the event is stored within the crystals. You can also receive information from almost any item. For instance, someone's cell phone carries the energy of the person who routinely uses it. This is what happens when someone who is adept at psychometry picks up information about a person by holding an article of their clothing. This happens as a result of the person's energy field altering or imprinting on the article of clothing. This subtle change of energy is picked up by the person holding the item.

Using Remote Viewing and astral travel to access information that will affect the lives of others puts new importance on these skills. A clear energy field helps you to obtain cleaner information when Remote Viewing or astral traveling, as you will not have a heavy filter that might dilute or alter the information flowing to you. Therefore, you can depend more on your information being correct.

How you connect with a specific soul signature has to do with intent. If I am to transmit thoughts or access information across a distance, I must recognize the correct signature before communication can take place.

Sending energy and communication from your soul signature to another person can be accomplished by just clearing your mind and focusing your intent. You have probably done this many times without thinking about it. We have all had situations where we thought about someone and then the phone rang and it was that exact person who was calling us. We can even communicate with our pets as well as our houseplants over a distance through clear focused intent.

By accessing the energy of an event that is stored at the location where the event took place, there is much information to be gathered. This is how much of the information was accessed by Michael and myself when working a murder or kidnapping case. In sending our consciousness into the earth at the location of a crime, we were able to obtain details of the events that took place there even if it happened many years prior to the viewing. I will explain this process further in the next chapter.

Eleven

A Spirit Ate My Homework

*"The only true wisdom is in knowing
you know nothing."*
Socrates.

Luna's Dream February, 2013
*There is a new electronic device that you hold
up to your third eye and it records your thoughts
and visions like a movie. Then you can hold it to
someone else's third eye and they will get the exact
information that you had in your mind's eye.*

It is said that many of our dreams are about problem solving. The February, 2013, dream seemed to be in answer to my concern of making my Remote Viewings precise and to be masterful at conveying the information that was being downloaded into my subconscious in such a way that I would have great accuracy. I felt deep responsibility to communicate my viewings so they would be interpreted correctly.

Many of the cases covered in this chapter have never been resolved and so I have not divulged many details from my viewings. Viewings that were submitted, the police departments were sometimes tossed aside or sometimes taken as valuable information. Accomplishing viewings for crimes can be a process that lacks reward. The viewings do not always provide the information that will assist the authorities in finding the perpetrator. Even if the information is valuable, it can still take years before an actual conviction is achieved. However, as the messenger, I do not feel it is up to me to filter the information. I forward whatever I get. I am the messenger.

Within the Remote Viewing class, Michael would give us homework and we would send our consciousness to the boxes located at Michael's home to access the targets and then write down aspects and draw pictures. We would then bring our notes to the next Wednesday night class and receive confirmation on the targets when Michael opened the boxes. Michael taught us many tools to use such as taking an "astral flashlight" with us if we needed light to see inside the dark box. We were also taught how to rise above the item, move around it to get a 360-degree view as well as manifesting an "astral finger" to tap on the item to see if the surface was hard or soft. Most helpful for me was sensing the vibration of the energy that the target was emitting. As time went on I became more and more proficient at identifying and communicating with the energy of the item. I could tell that a target made of metal had an energetic quality that I equated to a "ping" sound and I could sense that the energy flowed in a particular direction. A battery had a sharp and buzzy quality to it. Plastic had a "dead" quality to it; the energy did not move. I could feel the aliveness of a plant and the previous life force of a piece of animal fur or a feather. I was developing a tool box. Even colors had subtle energy differences. I could see shapes, feel textures and structures, sense light or dark contrast.

After attending two of Michael's weekly classes, I was lying on my bed accessing altered brain wave activity and getting ready to Remote View the homework boxes. As I entered deeper and deeper into trance I attempted to connect to one of the boxes.

Suddenly I felt the soul signature of another person within my consciousness. It was the energy of a young girl. I was intercepted by the spirit of a little girl! This was not supposed to happen! Michael mentioned nothing about this in class. Was it truly possible to be intercepted by a spirit when out in the astral planes? Somehow, I was now engaged in astral communication with a six-year-old girl whose spirit was floating around in the astral planes. I just wanted to do my homework. I wanted to get a clear picture of what was in the box, obtain the aspects, write them down on my paper and get some valuable feedback when I returned to class on Wednesday night. Persistently, the little girl's spirit blocked me from doing my homework and insisted that I pay attention to what she needed to tell me.

The trauma she had experienced began to unfold in my mind's eye like a video. She had been walking down a road that had tall pine trees on either side. There were houses that were set back from the road surrounded by lush grass. Everything looked very green; it must have been summer. I could see that she was wearing jogging pants. I saw the pants as blue or red and she had on a t-shirt. Her hair was light brown or dark blonde and somewhat short and her brown eyes were so expressive and bright. She told me her name was Liz Beth. She was upset. There had been some type of argument and she walked away down the road.

She had been kidnapped and murdered and she started to download information about the crime into my consciousness. I was assaulted by the thoughts and visions that she showed me. I was so UPSET and surprised. Who was this person who was invading my relaxed state of mind? Images and information came though at a rapid-fire pace. I tried to protest but she was not taking no for an answer. She had chosen me to take this important information to the police. I started drawing pictures and writing down everything that I could; recording the information. I kept seeing the words or digits: Nova III, Nova III. I was not certain if the digits III were Roman numerals or the letters I's or L's. Later, I would find out that this possibly meant Nora, Illinois. As my work on the case progressed I found out that she had been living in Joliet, Illinois at the time of her disappearance. Somehow this little girl's spirit had decided that I could help solve her crime. I didn't ask for it but I did receive the information. I barely slept that night. Liz Beth's spirit was with me all night. I felt her energy signature and the intense importance of this information. I laid in bed with tablet of paper and pen next to me. As the information flooded my brain, I feverishly wrote it all down, waking up from a light sleep several times to document the facts. Using the tools I had learned so far in my Remote Viewing classes, I sent my consciousness into the earth at the location of the crime to access the stored knowledge.

I saw his face. I perceived that he was slightly retarded, either from birth or from an accident that happened while he was a child which caused brain damage. I saw the car he drove, but I was not sure if that car was from the time of the crime or if it was now. I think she knew him. I saw where he lived. I saw identifying marks on his skin, tapped into his height and weight. I knew her body was disposed in a place different from the site of the murder. There were many more details that streamed through.

With little sleep, I could not concentrate. Liz Beth had consumed my heart and soul. It was as if she were my own daughter who had been missing and now after many, many years, I was receiving information on her death. I couldn't just let it go.

The next day, I dragged myself to work and tried to function in the office. Liz Beth continued to stay with me, giving me more and more information. I could not focus on my work. I did my best to hide my secret messenger from my employees and clients. In over my head and feeling distraught, I finally called Michael and told him what was happening. He left work immediately and showed up at my office. I explained in detail the events that had unfolded over the past twenty-four hours. I was relieved that Michael did not judge me. He did not look at me as if I had two heads. He seemed very interested. In fact, Michael did not de-value my Remote Viewing of this crime in any way. The earnest interest that he demonstrated helped me to feel confident divulging all the information.

As if Liz Beth had taken over my body, I stood up and moved to the white board hanging in my office. As if someone had taken control of my hand, a map of the crime scene appeared on the board. It was the bird's eye view of what I had received from Liz Beth; a map of the crime scene. I turned around and studied the look on Michael's face. I thought he would show signs of disbelief. As an insurance agent I had trained myself to read body language and facial expressions. Michael's look was one of interest and wonderment. He examined Liz Beth's map of lake, pier, and a big "X" where her death had occurred. Michael directed me to pull up the missing children's website, www.missingkids.org.

My heart was beating so hard I thought it would pop out of my chest and flop around on the desk. I searched the pictures quickly. *So many missing children!* Then I saw her. I felt my stomach drop to the floor as Liz Beth's intense brown eyes looked back at me from the website almost as if she was trapped in the computer. It was her! I felt validated. Liz Beth was real. This really did happen!

I looked at her name, *Oh! "Sarah Avon." Oh no! How could she tell me that her name was Liz Beth? Was this the right child?* I looked at her picture again. Yes, this was her... how could she give me the wrong name? Was all of the information wrong? I momentarily questioned everything she had told me. Then I saw her middle name, Elizabeth. *Yes! Of course, she was using a nickname derived from her middle name. It is her!* Maybe her family called her that, or maybe she decided to take on that name in the astral planes. It didn't matter. I knew it was her.

I could not breathe. My throat closed up. I wasn't just making this up. Liz Beth was a real little girl who had lived a real life and I was looking at her picture right now. All of the astral produced video that she had shown me the previous night was truly real. I could not hold back the tears any longer. I began to sob and sob. The tears flowed out of me from lack of sleep, from the chaos in my mind, from the heaviness of my responsibility that this little girl had placed on me.

I explained to Michael that I had not slept and that I could not function at work because little Liz Beth kept invading my thoughts, keeping me from focusing and sleeping. I wasn't sure how much longer I would be able to continue. I was depleted.

Michael looked at me with eyes that exuded compassion. He could tell I was almost at my breaking point. He then said in a confident tone of voice, "*First of all, let's not talk with anyone else about this right now. You don't want anyone else's thoughts or feelings to muddy up your communications with Liz Beth. Now, let's see if we can get you some rest and rejuvenation. There are two things happening here. You are in emotional turmoil because you are not putting up enough protection while interacting with her and her traumatic events. You know you don't have to experience all of the sound and the pain and the emotion. You can watch it as if it is on TV and use an astral remote to fast forward through anything that is difficult for you.*"

I felt great relief. I knew that asking Michael for help was the right thing to do and now he was demonstrating how well experienced he was and sharing valuable and easy-to- use tools with me.

He then taught me another new tool: Astral Toggle Switches. Knowing that I could quickly manifest anything with my intent in the astral planes, I could create Astral Toggle Switches and label them with titles such as "sound," "emotion," "vision," etc. Then, I could choose which ones I needed to turn on and which ones I could turn off. This tool of control I would use many times over the years while working emotionally draining targets.

So, I could re-enter this viewing and I could view the event without hearing her scream. If there were parts I did not want to see, I could turn those off also. The toggle switches were truly helpful to keep me focused on retrieving information about Liz Beth's disappearance while retaining my sanity.

Then Michael taught me about controlling when and where I would receive the information. He told me not to worry about being available for Liz Beth 24/7. I could let her know that, yes, I did want to receive the information and I did want to help her but she could not interrupt me at the office or while I was sleeping. I agreed to be available and ready to listen each night before I fell asleep and she agreed to wait until that time to download more information.

Michael became my mentor in this viewing. We discussed what type of information would be helpful to the Police to assist them in solving the crime. He also told me that he would do viewings on the perpetrator and that I could continue to work with Liz Beth's spirit and that he would then type up all the notes and submit them to the Will County Sheriff's office in Illinois.

By the time Michael left my office I felt comforted and grateful. I now had some tools and direction on how to proceed with Liz Beth. I spent the next few nights consumed with her communications. I carefully wrote down each detail. I drew maps and diagrams until there were no other facts available. I gave all of my information to Michael who submitted it, along with his viewings to the Will County Sheriff's Department on September 5, 2002. He included a cover letter that explained Remote Viewing to give some background to the department in case they had not interacted with Remote Viewers previously.

In reviewing my notes I had documented information from Liz Beth that gave me details on what was left at the crime scene, the type and color of vehicle the perpetrator drove, information on the criminal's marital status, what type of house he lived in and what type of jewelry he wore. There are many other details that were transmitted to me and all of it was provided to the sheriff's office.

We never heard from the Will County Sheriff's Department. Maybe they were not open to details that had been obtained in what they may have considered an unorthodox method. Or maybe they are still gathering enough of the right information to warrant an arrest. I feel deep disappointment to see that Liz Beth's photo is still on the missing children's website each time I check it. You will see her listed as Sarah Avon in Illinois. I do understand that even though Liz Beth provided me with a lot of information, it is most likely still not enough for a conviction.

As of today, this crime has not been solved.

If she had been allowed to live, Liz Beth would be forty-one years old now. Her murder was committed thirty-five years ago and so far she is still listed as a missing person.

Looking back at the events surrounding this first case, I realize that Liz Beth helped to bond Michael and me as a couple. This was important work and we learned a lot about each other during this time.

Weeks later, after we had completed our work on the Liz Beth case, I was surprised to be intercepted by her again. This time she introduced me to the spirit of another little girl who had been kidnapped and murdered. This child was Sandra Quintanar Brieno. Sandra was missing from Morales, Mexico. I worked this case eight separate times. I received information regarding the crime, the location, the perpetrator, and identifying marks on his body, and information on where her body was dumped. Michael also did one viewing on her case.

Michael submitted the information to El Paso, Texas police department on December 18, 2002 because, from the information that we were receiving from the astral planes, the perpetrator was living in the United States in that location.

Many times the information that is downloaded into my energy field is not specific enough but may trigger something for the detectives working the case.

Here is an excerpt from one of my viewings:

I see a landfill off a dirt road, within forty-five miles of a motorcycle shop. This is a dumping ground for commercial trash. The perpetrator used a pickup truck to dump the body but it was not his truck. He borrowed it. I think it is a Ford. License plate is blue with dark yellow numbers and letters. There is a hubcap missing from the driver's side rear wheel. Something in the back of the truck rattles while driving over a dirt road. The body is in two black plastic bags. The body is not severed, the bags are connected to each other. The road leads to the East. There are low sloping hills.

The picture unfolded for me like a movie. However, not all of the Information would be usable by the police department.

To complicate things even further, while I was working on the Sandra Brieno case, another little girl popped in who I will call Angelica Weir. I was getting a download of a lot of information from Liz Beth. Some of it was on her crime, some of it was for the two other little girls. Stress, confusion and the intensity of the responsibility were taking over my life. Also there was the issue of time folding over on itself.

Angelica was thirteen years old when she went missing. In working this case, I obtained information about her disappearance and Michael submitted it to the police. Working the Angelica Weir case was interesting because I could tell that she was still in her physical body. My viewing was less gut-wrenching. I got information on where she was and while I was connected to her spirit, I asked her to get back to her mother.

While writing this book, I could no longer find Angelica on the Missing Children's Website. I contacted the police department in Georgia, and also researched information in the archives of newspapers. I received an email back from a detective in Georgia on February, 11, 2016, stating that Angelica was back home with her mother. A happy ending!

In reviewing all the documents, I found a hand-written note from my Remote Viewing teacher, who later became my husband, stating *"I believe that you have been chosen by these children to be their spokesperson."*

A heaviness descended upon me at the time he wrote it and I felt a keen responsibility to make sure that my viewings were as perfect as I could possibly make them. I felt it was a mission for me to help the perpetrators get caught.

Here is an excerpt of one of the emails that I sent to Michael on August 22, 2002, just one month after joining the Remote Viewing class.

"As I was in alpha trying to connect to the transmission that Vickie (one of the RV students) was broadcasting, I got a really strong image of this guy and I decided to go with it to see where it would take me. Basically this is a kidnap, murder and necrophilia (sexual defilement of a corpse). I was viewing this information for over a half hour and I got a lot of details. I kept thinking that maybe my analytical mind was doing this because of all the missing kids (we have been working on) right now. But Liz Beth came in and she was insistent that I pay attention. I have pages written on this. Please see if you get anything so we can compare details. I don't know what I am supposed to do with this info...But I will try again tonight to see if I can get any more. Let me know if you get anything."

The confusion and the intensity says it all. I was driven to be out-of-body and connected to Liz

Beth's world for many hours each day. I feared that I would miss important information if I did not open myself up to the communications.

I was now having a difficult time going into the post office. I would see the photos of missing children hanging on the wall and I felt like they were reaching out to me. All of them! The burden of dealing with the difficult cases of missing children was taking its toll on me.

Another case we worked together was on Aarone Thompson from Colorado in 2005. This little girl had probably been dead for quite some time before the parents ever reported her as missing. The records show that she was missing since November 14, 2005. Our viewings were submitted to Detective Brian Hansen of the Aurora, Colorado Police Department on January 12, 2006. My viewing contained this information as well as other details:

Blue dress with white flowers, one tennis shoe. Large cottonwood tree by itself on South side of long straight road approximately forty-five minutes East of Aurora. Barbed wire fence, in "L" shape, high grasses. You will find her body there.

The Aurora Police Department contacted us regarding this case. They asked further questions after our viewings were submitted. Aarone was missing sometime between May, 2002 and November, 2005. The mother, Shelly Lowe, died of a heart attack during investigations. The father, Aaron Thompson was arrested in September, 2009. Mr. Thompson was initially charged with sixty counts of child abuse, conspiracy and other crimes. He was found guilty of thirty-one of the charges including child abuse involving the use of a baseball bat, child abuse leading to death, conspiracy, concealing a dead body, abuse of a corpse and many other terrible offenses against his children. He is now in prison sentenced to 114 years. Sadly, as of the publication of this book, Aarone's body has not been recovered.

In March, 2014 we worked the missing person's case of Nathaniel Tallman of Lafayette, Colorado. Typically when working a target such as this one, viewers including myself, access the target many times, getting pieces of the puzzle each time. So a target may be worked several times over a period of many days. As I worked this target, images came through quickly of a drug deal that went bad. Nathaniel had been missing since January 23, 2014. I picked up a connection to Wyoming and knew he was no longer living. Before we had a chance to submit our information to the authorities, his body was found in Lusk, Wyoming with a bullet wound and the details outlined in the newspaper confirmed my viewings.

The Keddie Murders took place in 1981. The Keddie Resort is located in a remote area Northeast of Sacramento. Sue Sharp was staying in cabin 28 with her fifteen-year-old son and twelve year old daughter. All three of them were murdered as well as the son's seventeen-year-old friend. Sue Sharp's two youngest sons and one of their friends were in the cabin also at the time of the murders in a bedroom apparently asleep and were unaware of the crime taking place.

In April, 2010 we were contacted by someone close to us that knew the Sharp family, to do a viewing on this event. This was a brutal murder of four people. The murder weapon was a hammer. As of the writing of this book, the murder case is still a cold case file. This was a particularly difficult case for me to work due to the extreme violence that was involved.

As this book nears publication, I was sent an update that the file had been re-opened after all these years. A request was made for me to accomplish more viewings and transmit them to the police. I am not certain this is a case that I can reconnect with at this time. It is emotionally draining and I have tried to retire from this part of my job description. This and other murder cases have taken their toll on me. It is emotionally draining to work these cases no matter how much help I may be able to provide, and I need to back away.

Not all missing persons' cases had to do with murder. Sometimes there was a person missing who was known to be living. Over a period of years we worked a target of a missing child in India. We worked this target in 2010, 2011, 2013 and again in 2014. I will not put her real name here since she is still living. I will just call her Sasha. We used a target number similar to 519872. It was typical for Michael to give us a target number and not a name. This way we could eliminate what is called analytical overlay which could bias our viewings.

Sasha had been taken from her family in India at age two and was being raised by the perpetrators. Over a period of seven years the biological parents had searched for their child. I worked this case many times with good results, describing the school she was attending, and the general location and description of the home where she was living. When we were asked to do our final viewing, I got a very clear message from Sasha's spirit that she was happy where she was. I know it is tragic for the biological family to not have their child returned to them and I certainly did not have any indication that they were unfit parents. However, at age nine, the child did not even remember that she had a different set of parents and I was getting the clear message that taking her from her current situation and getting her back to her biological family was actually going to be more harmful for her. Honoring the greater good, I had to pull myself from the viewing. I have no regrets that I did not complete that last viewing.

There were many other targets that we worked over the years for missing people, missing pets and missing jewelry. I would like to say that I am officially retired from working any of the missing persons' cases. Unless, of course, I get intercepted while out in the astral planes.

Twelve
Remote Viewing Terrorists

"Pass through the wall....."
"Psychic Warrior" by David Morehouse.

Due to the sensitive nature of this chapter, I have substituted fictitious names, target numbers and omitted many details. I am presenting the subject matter as I remember it to the best of my ability. However, some of the specifics have been changed to protect the privacy of individuals as well as to keep the untrained from attempting to access astral secure locations and information.

There was a knock on the door.

Michael and I moved in together in January, 2003. We had taken up residence in a ranch-style home on a thirty-two acre parcel of land at the top of Golden Gate Canyon in Colorado. The home was accessible by two miles of dirt road. Someone just showing up without calling ahead was not typical. As I opened the door, I saw two men dressed in black suits, white shirts, black ties and black plastic-rimmed sunglasses. "Is Michael Van Atta home?" one of them asked in a monotone.

His face was expressionless and all I could think of was the movie Men In Black. How odd that these two characters would just appear at our door. There was no car in the driveway. It was as if they had just materialized out of thin air.

Michael went outside with the two men for about twenty minutes. I was curious why these men had traveled up to the top of the mountain to have a private meeting with him. Once back inside, I questioned Michael. His response was this: *"I did some undercover work for the government and there are people that keep track of my location, and check in on me from time to time."* I probably should have asked more questions but I could tell that Michael did not want to discuss it further at that point. Thinking that someday I would get some background information about these guys, I let the subject drop.

After Michael died, I found a list of activities that he had detailed titled: "In Life We Leave Behind Tracks on the Fabric of Reality." Michael listed his "tracks" as follows:

1) He received an Eagle Scout award in 1964.

2) He served in Vietnam as a Staff Sergeant, Airborne Ranger and was awarded two Bronze Stars for combat and seven other combat ribbons, Presidential Citations and Air Medal.

3) He completed two Marine Corps marathons, one civilian marathon and seven triathlons.

4) In 1980 he worked undercover operations for the FBI wearing a wire taped to his back into meetings with government officials to record bribes that were being offered.

5) In 1980, in conjunction with a CIA covert team he dug under the wire fence surrounding a prison camp in Southeast Asia and took pictures of Americans being held against their will in the prison.

6) In 1981, he led a group of (then) current and former intelligence officers reviewing CIA and DIA (Defense Intelligence Agency) files containing thousands of debriefings of witnesses who reported feeding, guarding and providing medical care to live American POWs.

7) He managed twenty-three operations in the 1980's and 1990's wherein teams of Americans went into foreign countries (Russia, China, Vietnam, Cambodia, North Korea and Cuba) seeking evidence of live Americans being held against their will.

Michael was not your average guy. He had certainly left his tracks on the fabric of reality. He had not talked about these events to me but I know that he had to wait for the information to be de-classified. However, on the document he left for me to find after his death, he did leave references that can be researched, and I have listed them at the back of this book.

During the years we lived in that house in the rural and remote foothills of Colorado, it was obvious that our phones were tapped. Loud clicking sounds were heard on the line while we made phone calls. There were other strange events, such as a cigar-shaped UFO sighting which was reported by me to the local MUFON chapter using the name of "Celeste."

Only five months after we had met in Remote Viewing class, we both left our spouses and moved in together. Michael was my teacher; and our work on missing children as well as our memories of past lives together created a strong bond that was undeniable. When we were not at our traditional jobs, our focus was on Remote Viewing and astral travel.

Remote Viewing is basically a military term for a type of astral travel. Project Grill Flame was formalized in 1978 at Fort Meade, Maryland. It became a $20 million project which was later minimized and by 1990 the military was spending just $500,000 per year and supposedly terminated the program in 1995. It is not the focus of my book to teach you the history of the Remote Viewing project in the U.S. I just wanted to give you a small introduction so you have an idea of what it is about. There are many books that have been written by military Remote Viewers on the topic.

David Morehouse was a soldier in the United States Army. After a head injury, he was visited by an angel and gifted with psychic abilities and moved to the Remote Viewing project. He later left the service and began teaching Remote Viewing.

Morehouse defines Remote Viewing as:

"The learned ability to transcend space and time, to view persons, places or things remote in space-time; to gather and report information on the same."

There are only small differences between Remote Viewing and astral travel as far as I am concerned. However, if you ask military Remote Viewers, they would probably tell you that psychic abilities and God have nothing to do with the process. I have always seen Remote Viewing as a process of obtaining non-local information using a strict protocol that was created by the U.S. military. Astral travel, on the other hand, can be a more experiential process and does not have strict protocols.

Michael attended workshops taught by David Morehouse on the island of St. John in the U.S.Virgin Islands before I met him. Using what he learned from David Morehouse, as well as his out of body experience, he began teaching. When I took Michael's Remote Viewing class, he had previously taught just one series of classes with a group of about thirty students. I was in the second series of classes.

I do not proclaim to be a military Remote Viewer. The United States military used a lot of protocols that to me are cumbersome and unnecessary. I know that for the military to endorse something that sounds like psychic abilities, and spend $20 million, they needed to make it structured and measurable. In strict military Remote Viewing protocols, every step is followed carefully including declaring analytical overlay, drawing and probing an ideogram and even using a specific type of pen, a Pilot Uni-ball pen, black of course!

As my years progressed with Michael, we settled into a life that was not typical. We would be eating dinner and the phone would ring and suddenly we would drop everything in the interest of national security just like Jamie Lee Curtis and Arnold Schwarzenegger in the movie True Lies. This movie resonated with us as husband and wife living what seemed to be mundane lives, but a phone call could send them into the world of spies and intrigue.

Michael belonged to a group that I will call REVEL. This is a group of advanced civilian Remote Viewers who work targets that after a few layers of filters, end up in the hands of the United States government.

One night while eating dinner, we had a phone call from Nina. Nina was our contact person for REVEL. I would later find out that she was the head of a highly classified project that was authorized by a government intelligence agency. The Remote Viewing requests worked by the REVEL group were submitted to civilians who were authorized by a governmental agency that is masterful in the art of encryption. It's no surprise that there are layers of protection between us and the actual government entities who ask for and ultimately receive the information.

Michael had been recruited by REVEL through the American Society of Dowsers several years before I met him. Nina later told me that when she first spoke with him she could tell he had been involved in government intelligence work by the way he talked. There is a certain language that is spoken by those who have done undercover work. He was considered to be an A+++ viewer, possibly due to the head injury he had suffered as a child. Many people who develop psychic abilities have had a head injury that opens them up to receiving information from the collective unconscious.

Within a year, I was accepted to work the targets. Looking back, I am certain that the members of REVEL must have Remote Viewed me to decide if I should be let in. I always took the work seriously and I felt keen responsibility to do my best, as typically the safety of our country and our government was at stake.

Most times we would work a blind target. We were given a number and would not have any idea what the target number applied to. In this way, we would be protected from "analytical overlay." Although I had been trained by Michael with his version of protocols, I knew that I was more of an intuitive than a Remote Viewer.

On this particular phone call, Nina told us there was a nuclear suitcase bomb that had entered the United States. We were to locate it and provide all the information we could gather.

We were in the middle of eating our dinner but of course we dropped everything and began to work the target. This was a priority. The information that we provided to Nina could save hundreds of thousands of lives. This was not a viewing we could postpone.

I began working target number 4629, 1136. I followed Michael's version of the traditional military protocols. Name, date, time all at the top of the blank unlined page, using my black Pilot Uni-Ball pen.

Then I remembered that I had not put protection around myself. Protection is something the military did not teach their viewers, as far as I know. I was taught by a spiritual teacher in Colorado to protect my energy field. In working a target such as this one, I felt I needed to put up protection in case of psychic attack from the terrorists. I placed a thick shield of white light around myself by projecting it out from my heart space and solidified it with a protective outer shell.

I declared any analytical overlay that could keep me from having a clean viewing and dropped into a deep alpha state. I wrote the target number 4-6-2-9, 1-1-3-6 and drew my ideogram. The ideogram is a scribbled line extending off from the last digit of the target number. It is drawn as an impulse or reflexive action and represents connection to the information that is contained within the actual target. Once drawn, the information is unlocked by probing it with your pen. I began to probe my ideogram.

The intensity level was building in my energy field. I felt a heightened awareness, super sensitivity. I turned on all of my intuitive and Remote Viewing antennas. Dropping into an altered brain wave level makes everything seem sharper and more vivid. Colors, sounds, smells, everything is heightened and especially the connection to the collective unconscious; the location of all energetic information. Similar to the "Cloud" internet data storage, the collective unconscious is an etheric data storage location where all knowledge of past, present and future is stored.

Within this library of information there is a "Help Desk" that some Remote Viewers have access to. This Help Desk is an astral location that exists to keep viewers on task and to guide them in ways that will help humanity in general. I accessed the "Help Desk" asking for any and all assistance that was available on this target.

Probing the ideogram with my pen, information began to flow and I began to get aspects of the target. I picked up the energy of steel and felt the frequencies of a deep gray color... charcoal gray. I tapped on the object with my "astral finger" and perceived it as hard and flat and metallic and cold.

I sent my consciousness up above the target about thirty feet and I realized that I was at a container ship in a harbor. I moved around the target 360 degrees to see it from all angles. I raised up even farther, this time a few hundred feet up, to access some identifiable landmarks to determine what harbor the ship was in. I kept going up higher and higher and then realized that I was viewing the East coast of the United States, pinpointing the target near Boston.

I felt fear start to creep into my awareness. *Stay focused! Stay focused! Don't let your emotions get in the way. Get the information that is needed to get this threat taken care of. Don't get bogged down with insignificant details. Get the information that will help to resolve the issue.*

I was able to actually see the ship. The target was on as I began to "zoom" my consciousness back in for a closer view. I counted ships over from a pier, I drew pictures, I saw which container it was in. The energy from the target was intense. I was on edge. I felt pressure to make sure that my viewings were perfect. I felt that many lives were in my hands and that I was partly responsible for the outcome of what would take place. *Intense, intense! Stay focused! Don't get distracted.*

I moved around the ship and saw a series of letters and numbers on the side near the bow. It can be very difficult to read numbers or letters when Remote Viewing. I felt a lot of pressure about being right. There was a lot at stake in this viewing. What if I provided incorrect information? Or even worse, what if I read the mind of another viewer who was also wrong? That had happened to me before in our Remote Viewing club meetings with another viewer. She and I routinely sat near each other. We would both access the same target information and we would both be wrong. It was good for a laugh but this was not the time for humor.

Refocus. I wrote the target number again and scribbled a new ideogram. In probing the ideogram, I focused on reading the numbers on the side of the ship. I4NH....I was able to get some of the information. I wrote down the digits I was getting. There were other numbers or letters but I could not get them. Maybe this will at least help. I cannot hold back information just because it might not be complete.

Then I raised up above the row of container ships with a bird's eye view so I could get a better view of the location. I took the target number again and scribbled the ideogram. *Probe it. Probe it. Get more information. I need to be perfect.* I felt extreme pressure to get the right information.

My energy level was so intense and so focused. I lost track of my surroundings. I felt disconnected from y physical body. All of my consciousness was with the ship. I got aspects... metal, cold, gray, box like. *Okay, I already had that information, what else? What else? What else could I get that would be pertinent?*I hated working these intense targets. I felt the extreme burden of having the future of our country on my back. I know that the reason there are many people working the same target because Remote Viewing is an inexact science. So feeling such pressure was unwarranted but I still felt it. After exhausting all information that I could obtain, I pulled myself back into my physical body and sat back, feeling exhausted from the magnitude of the situation. I was back in the physical world feeling off-kilter and on edge.

As I looked over at Michael, he came back into his body with a big smile. *"Why are you so happy?"* I asked, thinking that I must have worked a different target. *"I dismantled it,"* he stated *"I used remote effecting and I rendered the suitcase bomb unusable."* That was Michael all right, always a step ahead of me.

Another time we got a call that a terrorist had just crossed the Canadian border into the United States and our job was to locate him so he could be found and detained. Knowing this to be a volatile target, I surrounded myself with white light. Following the military protocols as I had been trained, I set up my page, wrote my target number and scribbled my ideogram trailing off from it and probed it for information.

I could see his face. I wrote down the descriptive aspects but did my best to stay disconnected from him and his energy. It is a fine line to stay disconnected and to still receive information. I tapped into the energy signature of this person. He felt angry but also empty, almost as if he had been programmed, like a computer. I wrote all of my descriptive aspects down regarding his appearance. I saw the car he was in. I got the color and shape. His intensity was so strong that I was having a difficult time staying disconnected from his energy and at the same time remain connected enough to receive more details. I got as much information as I could about his location and wrote it down. I submitted all the information that I received.

When doing viewings such as this it would be great to have feedback but most of the time the only positive feedback is NOT reading anything in the newspaper or hearing of any extreme events on the news reports. This was typically the case when working the government targets. There are many things that are happening behind the scenes that the public is not aware of. I think of this as hysteria control.

Many of the targets that we worked though REVEL were blind targets. In other words, we would receive a number but no other information on the target. There were many targets I did not work. I would tap into the energy and if it felt too volatile or I was feeling too fragile that day I would bow out. Or Michael would tell me he was going to work a target but did not think I should get involved and I honored his direction. He knew that I was an empath and susceptible to the energy of the targets even though I put up a lot of protection. Michael worked all of the targets given to him and submitted them to Nina.

By the time Michael and I met, the government, prompted by the 9/11 attacks that happened in 2001, had their own groups set up and were using REVEL less frequently than before. So my involvement was quite minimal compared to his. We were filling in the gaps and still working targets with REVEL but less frequently. Most of the targets we worked were level fours and fives. I am still contacted to work some targets once in a while but it is not as frequently as it was between 2002 and 2007.

And so this was our life while Michael and I were together for twelve years. When we were not working targets or teaching Remote Viewing, we were helping others through alternative healing.

Thirteen
Astral Romance

"The energy which underscores sex is the energy which underscores life; which is life! The feeling of attraction and the intense and often urgent desire to move toward each other, to become one, is the essential dynamic of all that lives. I have built it into everything.
It is inbred, inherent, inside All That Is."
"Conversations with God" by Neale Donald Walsch.

After our first connection within this lifetime at Remote Viewing class, Michael and I had experienced a knowing of prior lifetimes together. We also knew we were reunited to do important work together that would touch the lives of others. There was a power that was greater than ourselves that was drawing us together. There were obstacles to overcome but none seemed to be too great. For us, the most challenging obstacle was that we were married to other people and even that was not enough to keep us apart.

Destined to be together, we started a process of sending our soul signatures to each other's homes to see if we would be aware of our presence. We tried this experiment mostly in the evening and since neither of us was actually sleeping in the same bedrooms as our spouses, we had the opportunity to try out the process of sending our soul signatures to meet with each other without interruption.

Sprawled out across my bed in a relaxed state preparing to do some meditation, I felt Michael's presence in the room. In fact, I had a knowing that he was sitting in the chair in the corner of the room. I grinned and waved. It was a reflexive reaction that took no thought. I was not sure if his soul signature would acknowledge that I waved to him or not. I looked at the clock and documented the time; it was 9:17 p.m..

The following day we compared notes. Michael said he came to see me and he was in the corner of the room. The timing was off however; he thought he was there just before 9:00 p.m.. Without prompting from me, he acknowledged that I had waved at him. We discussed how time moves differently in the astral planes and that possibly I was picking up on the energy imprint that he had left in the room before I had even entered it. Also since in the astral there technically is no time – time is a manmade system that only serves our physical world – it is possible to experience past, present and future all at the same time within the astral planes. Removing myself from the restrictions of time was another lesson learned from Michael.

My first sexual experience with Michael was in the astral planes and happened spontaneously.

Here is my perception of what happened that night.

Luna's Journal Entry
September 10, 2002

I was doing my Remote Viewing homework tonight, sending my consciousness into the wooden boxes that were located at Michael's home to retrieve aspects of the targets. Achieving an alpha brainwave state and leaving my physical body behind, I was intercepted by an entity that felt familiar. Our astral bodies merged and I realized that this was a sexual experience that was taking place! It was exciting and energizing and like nothing I had ever experienced. The entity seemed to be the soul signature of Michael. Could it be that I had sex with my Remote Viewing teacher???? Is he aware of what happened? Did he initiate it? So many questions! How am I supposed to get the answers for these crazy questions? I am going to wait for class next week and see if he acts differently around me......

Then the following night it happened again. And again. Each night I would look forward to these loving encounters before doing my homework for class. Finally Wednesday rolled around and it was time to go to class. I was filled with anticipation. I paid closer attention to how I dressed, making sure my hair and makeup were perfect. I walked into class and took my seat. Michael was focused on teaching but kept looking at me and smiling. I did not have the nerve to approach him. Okay, I was all right with that, I went home and went back out of body for more interludes with "The Entity." This continued for another week.

I was pretty sure that it was Michael with whom I was having this secret affair. My husband knew I was taking Remote Viewing classes but he had no idea what was happening outside of the physical world. I truly enjoyed the astral sex experience. In my early fifties at the time, I loved how there were no physical limitations and I became consumed with the act of astral sex. It was on my mind all the time. I was out of body for longer and longer periods of time. It truly became a way to escape a marriage that had gone bad. It seemed that each time I went out into the astral planes, Michael would be there waiting for me. We would have wonderful, loving sexual interactions and then we would each return to our celibate married lives.

As time passed I realized that Michael was flirting with me more and more after class but he would also talk about his wife, who was a well-known psychic. I was confused. I knew that I was going to eventually have to confront him about our astral encounters. Michael and I had been developing a friendship in this lifetime with our work on the Liz Beth case but the astral interludes took our friendship to another level. How was I supposed to approach him about this absurd subject? What if I was making it all up? Or worse, what if it was happening but with some entity that did not reside in a body I knew! After a couple weeks, I decided that I would just put it out there and if he thought I was insane, well, I would just deal with that and return to my astral boyfriend and try to find out who he was.

One night after class, to my surprise, Michael asked me if I wanted to get a bite to eat. We went to a small restaurant and I knew it was time for "The Discussion." Not knowing how to initiate the discussion, I threw out a comment about our past lives together. I hoped that somehow this would open up the conversation about our astral affairs. It did not work. He just let out a nervous laugh and I did not pursue it.

Another week went by. It was driving me nuts. I just knew it had to be him but as an astral-travel novice, I did not trust all of the impressions I was getting. We found ourselves alone after class standing in the class room. I knew it was time to attempt another try at "The Discussion." I was nervous. I was afraid he would say that he didn't know what I was talking about. Trying to formulate the question in my mind, all of a sudden Michael said, *"You have something important that you need to talk to me about."*

Okay... here goes nothing! I blurted out, *"I feel that you and I have been having a sexual relationship in the astral planes and I want it to continue."* Oh my God... he must think I am off my nut! *"I know that you are married and I am married but I really want this relationship to continue and I need to know how you feel about it!"* There I said it! Now what? Say something...........say SOMETHING!

The smile on Michael's face was welcoming and nurturing and full of love. I was so relieved. He had been there all along. Then he shared with me a specific manifestation he had been working on long before he met me.

He wrote the following on December 13, 2001:

Returning to my body from trance, I write down my desire to have an astral relationship. To explore and experience love in the astral planes in close proximity to God and God's pure and unconditional love.

The following day, Michael sent me this email:

"It makes sense to me. I know what you mean and yes I have been there with you. I worked at manifesting this situation many, many months before we even met! I dropped into a quiet space and released my request to the Universe. I know that once you ask, you forget about it. You release it from your attachment to the goal and allow God to create the situation in the right way in your life. I did that with a request on a piece of paper spelling out exactly what I wanted - setting it aside for a few days and then tearing it up and thrusting it into the Universe. I knew that my request would be heard and it would be answered and then YOU FELL FROM THE SKY! An answer to my Universal request. That's how it works!"

The miracle of manifesting something on the physical plane begins as a thought form. Many times putting the goal or wish in writing also helps to clarify it and communicate it to the

Universe. If the thought or wish begins with an analytical focus that is charged with emotion, it involves a combination of brain and heart energies working together. The thought form is solidified on the etheric level and communicated to the Divine and change begins to take place in the invisible world of energy, later to be manifested on the physical plane when the time is right.

Michael's wish of manifestation was written six months before we met and almost ten months before we began our intimate relationship in the astral planes. So after finally having the conversation and our sharing of experiences, our astral love affair rose to a higher level with openness and trust and secrecy. By joining our higher frequency astral bodies, we were able to experience the passion and pure loving feelings that are interwoven with the Divine. And so, our astral sexual affair became astral love. By acknowledging and honoring the special relationship, it now began to grow exponentially.

We decided to come up with a secret signal that our astral bodies or soul signatures could demonstrate so we were certain that we were meeting up with each other and not some other energy that was wandering around in the astral planes. This helped me feel more confident about meeting in the astral planes since my first few times out, I was not certain that it was truly Michael I was meeting. Our signal was a show of palm chakras with glowing golden hearts radiating outward.

Later on we would become adept at recognizing each other's soul signature as well as those of deceased loved ones, and others that we would meet in the etheric planes, such as Edgar Cayce.

We created an astral address where we could meet much like a target number. We used a six digit number which here I will call 173371. By assigning a number and setting up our own astral location, we could put up protection and create a sacred space that was just for us. Then, going into trance, we could send our consciousness to the location to have experiences. An astral location was already a tool that we had been using. Many Remote Viewers use an astral "Help Desk" with a specific astral target number or astral address. Now we had a new astral location with a specific address that was our private meeting place.

My consciousness would find its way to our astral location which we thought of as a sacred space in the shape of an orb of energy. I arrived at the location and manifested an astral hand which made the secret signal. Michael was already there. I recognized his energy signature immediately. His signature was always happy and vibrant and full of child-like wonderment and unconditional love. Now, I wish I had asked him to describe how he perceived my soul signature. I guess he would have said happy, vibrant and passionate. I felt his energy signature approaching mine. He produced an astral hand showing the secret gesture or mudra. I felt comfortable and relaxed once we completed our secret greeting. I returned the gesture. It was all going according to plan and that helped me to feel safe and confident. We basked in the energy of each other within this space, creating a unique energy that was the combination of the two of us.

We began leaving each other gifts at the astral location by manifesting an item with our thoughts and placing the soul signature of that item into our location. The other person could go to the location and "retrieve" the item. Michael would leave me the soul signature of a rose or other appropriate item. I would then go out to the sacred location and report back to Michael with information of what I had retrieved. He would then give me confirmation or feedback. This was a cool way for me to sharpen my skills. I also left gifts for him like crystals or other energetic or sacred items.

Our meetings, however, were not always perceived as a joining of astral bodies and sometimes not the optimum experience.

Luna's Journal Entry
November 19, 2002
I go to our astral sanctuary to meet with Michael. We greet each other with our hand signals and soul signature confirmation. I am overwhelmed with emotion. We connect but this time he seems distracted.

Email from Michael to Luna November 19, 2002

"Where were you? I was at our location but you were not."

Well, I was there, and I thought he was not. I think this was like having static on the line or being "out of pocket" with a cell-phone call. I call it astral confusion. Maybe the timing was wrong? That made no sense as there is no time in the astral planes. Time is nothing and everything. It is a manmade system that helps us keep our appointments here on earth. I was never able to figure out what happened on November 19th.

Luna's Journal Entry
November 22, 2002, morning

Michael and I enter our sanctuary and we start to get creative with our hand signal. We come together to exchange our soul signature recognition. I read this as a connection to my twin flame that my spirit has searched for and finally found. I accept the energy of five very slow deep penetrations from Michael. The penetration is seductive. I am glowing. I offer him delicate nibbles on parts of his astral body. I tease him and take my time. We both know that the second we are ready, we can join or inter-mesh our astral bodies and achieve orgasm instantly so we work at extending time until we are ready. We savor it. Then as we join, the energy exchange takes place. A sound of ommm vibrates throughout our sacred space. It resonates through us in shockwaves, reminding us of the Close Encounters movie. It is a loud sound, pulsating in rhythmic waves. My physical body arches in climax and I return to my room and realize physical confirmation of the event.

Luna's Journal Entry
November 22, 2002, nighttime

I approach our sanctuary and we exchange our hand signal from a distance. We move closer and show our recognition of soul signatures. Our astral bodies "dip in" and the flood of emotion overcomes me. I realize how much I have missed being with him from other lifetimes – lifetimes that included intense physical loving relationships. My soul has longed for his for who knows how many decades. My heart aches with joy to be with him. I show as golden light and so does he. We step together and our light becomes white and pure consciousness. This is an experience that is beyond verbal description.

Luna's Journal Entry
November 30, 2002

I project my spirit body out of my physical body and I am dancing and pivoting before Michael, whose astral body is reclining in the same room. He joins me in the etheric dance and off we go to our astral sanctuary. The colors, vibrations and sounds are vivid and heavenly. Then I realize there is a circle of spirit guides, or high frequency beings, in our sacred place. I get a download of information, a psychic hit, that they are there to share gifts and guidance with us. They are also there to gather energy that has taken on its own life from the synergy of the love that flows between the two of us. After a time, the spirit beings leave our space and we make astral love for over an hour. Returning to our physical bodies, we make love again on the earth plane and then discuss our astral experience. We are aware that the spirit guides have told us that we are together to help make the world a better place. To teach the process of astral love-making to help many people who are disfigured, imprisoned, or removed from their loved ones. We are to help others to experience love in the astral planes with their partners adding a new dimension of love and nurturing to others who are living without it.

Over a period of four months we continued to meet at 173371. As time moved on our relationship intensified quickly. It was becoming more and more difficult for us to be apart in the three dimensional world and we were both trying to figure out the confusing and complicated process of leaving our spouses. At least we were able to meet in the astral temple we had created and the energy was hot and steamy between us. Sexual energy within the astral planes is extremely powerful and primal and is better experienced than described. Out-of-body sexual interactions are much more intense than physical urges. There is a direct exchange of energies that is not filtered by the ego or the analytical mind, or physical limitations getting in the way.

I vividly remember one of the times we made love in the early stages of our relationship in the astral planes. We had expanded the astral temple to a large area where we could move great distances but still remain within the sacredness and safety of our temple walls. We were flying about, laughing and swooping and hovering. We were like a couple of children, experimenting with newly found experiences. Michael kept morphing his astral body to see what I liked. First he manifested a physical body with toned muscles and tight buns. He was being playful. I responded by producing a curvy, healthy, fit body. We grinned at each other and locked our astral gazes.

Next Michael started changing the size and shape of his penis asking me, *"Do you like this?"* showing off a rather long neon-glow-in-the-dark green member. *"How do you like this?"* now changing it to a fatter laser-white chunk with a flashing red tip. *"Shorter and wider? What is the perfect size and shape that you like? In the astral planes all things are possible!"*

Michael continued by changing the color to strobing rainbow colors spiraling from the base to the tip and sparkles swirling up around it. He was certainly a creative person and I was laughing so hard that I almost popped back into my physical body. We were enjoying the freedom of escaping our physical bodies. Manifesting anything in the astral planes was easy. A mere change of thought or emotion can manifest something because of being in the pure energy of the Creator. Within our sacred space, the merging of energies as each major chakra reached out to the corresponding chakra on the other astral body in an explosion of energy was amazing.

What is it like to merge astral bodies? Well if you can imagine merging with God and having a cosmic orgasm that is the best way I can describe it. Making love in the astral planes is like nothing I have ever experienced within my physical body. It is etheric and full of God's love and so complete. There is no wanting of things fitting together more perfectly. Or wishing something would be touched in a certain way but having the awkwardness of describing it to your partner. There is only the fullness of pure love and the integration of two God-like beings coming together. Your astral body is one of pure God energy and so is your partner's. Each person is merging with God. The coming together of these two energies is indescribable. It is like God making love with God.

Luna's Journal Entry
September 22, 2002

Michael and I decide to journey to our astral location at the same time to see what will take place.

Lime Jello... When I approach our site 173371, this time it takes on the look of shimmering, pulsating lime Jello... I still knew it was our site. How? The same way that I know that Michael is Michael when I see him in the astral. Our Astral Sanctuary has a soul signature of its own which feels familiar after so many visits.

I slip inside the lime Jello sanctuary. Michael is there with a big grin on his face. Instead of doing the secret hand signal. He has his index finger pointing upward and on it he is spinning a pair of black lace astral panties that I had gifted him at one point in time. So we laugh. This is a typical first connection in the astral. His sense of humor shows through and we often start with a giggle.

We face each other with what appears to be ten to twelve inches between us. Our chakras are sending energy back and forth to connect our thoughts, and our feelings. This is our way of saying "How have you been? What frame of mind are you in?" An astral communication of "How's it going?"

There are waves of energy coming through the lime Jello and we feel it pulsating our astral bodies, like standing in the ocean and feeling the tide move you. Our astral energies have become somewhat similar and so the exchange is not as intense as it was in the beginning. When we first started meeting like this in the astral planes, there was a much more intense exchange of energies as the frequencies rushed to fill in and balance the differences between the two of us. Instead, we exchange energy and have what I refer to as an astral orgasm within seconds. The encounter is on a much more spiritual level than it was when we first started these etheric encounters. The astral orgasm can best be described as waves of beautiful energy radiating outward from our co-joined astral bodies. Although it is a little less intense than the first few *times our energy bodies connected, it is still very sensual and I can tell that my physical body is responding. My physical body experiences the orgasm at the same time as my astral body; both convulsing.*

An email from Michael
September 22, 2002

I arrived at our Astral Sanctuary within minutes of projection. I sense the presence of my partner traveling with me to the Sanctuary. We are holding hands as we enter our sacred space. Once inside I immediately see her personality in holographic depth. With layers of thin differences like a piece of Selenite (a translucent, striated crystal) that has been peeled into very thin layers, but each layer is an aspect of her. It is multifaceted and she has aspects of her uniqueness that I have witnessed but in the mundane distractions of life, I had never paid attention to before. All of her personality unique traits were being displayed before me in layers. This was a wonderful and beautiful display of openness in which there is a total outpouring of her very fine vibrations that are all different parts of her thinking, her personality and her way of being. She is coming forward to me as herself, her being, her soul and displaying her depth and openness. I enjoy this encounter of trust and openness more than any other in the astral that I have experienced with her to date. I leave her a few items to find in the sanctuary... images of my worldly life and I hope she explores the sanctuary to find these things of meaning about me. Our energies connect with pulsating closeness as we enjoy each other's spirit bodies. There is a sharing of information that is passed between our souls. I return to the physical and find my partner, who is lying beside me. She is moaning with sexual pleasure but we are not physically touching. We both come back into our physical bodies and open our eyes, look at each other and smile. We then share our memories of our astral experiences.

How could we both leave our bodies at the same time and arrive at our sanctuary and have such different experiences? Some might think that we were making this up. However, for those who are adept at astral projection, they are aware that time means nothing in the astral planes. Past, present and future all happen at once and so even though it appeared that we left together, we obviously did not arrive at the sanctuary at the same time. There are an infinite number of possibilities that we could have experienced since all of time happens at once.

Luna's Journal Entry
October 1, 2002

We enjoy the waves of energy, we exchange life force through our chakras. This time we begin without an actual merging of astral bodies. Extending out from there, as our energies mix, they reach out to each other. As they finally touch, the energy shifts and the colors within our astral bodies change and swirl back into them.

When we have both achieved our astral orgasms, the inside of our sanctuary starts to "snow" with opalescent globes. The globes are the size of tangerines. They are moving slowly as if they are large snowflakes floating down through the space. Michael catches one and puts it to his third eye. His astral body absorbs it. It is a piece of knowledge from the Divine. We start catching our opalescent God-knowledge tangerines and put them to our third eyes and absorb them. Each one feels fulfilling and energizing. I am surprised at how simple the meaning of each energy orb is; "Joy," "Hugs," "Contentment," etc. I thought they would be profound. Then I get the message from somewhere: "The profound IS simple... that is why it is not recognized by most."

Michael puts his hand up to his third eye and "regurgitates" a globe and hands it to me and says, "Here, try this one!" I take the globe from him and put it to my third eye and absorb it. I realize that this is a special globe for us to share. Something within the globe tells me that this one is for the synergy that happens when we are together so I pay particular attention to what it is..... This globe's message is "Create." We look at each other and smile, the smile of recognition, of inner knowing. Then we put our astral bodies together and create a mandala of many colors. My energy is a deep red and Michael's is a pure turquoise with golden flecks.

As we interact there is a swirling of the colors creating a beautiful movement within a mandala that symbolizes the Divine knowledge that we received today. Our energy bodies began to swirl and merge with each other there are sparks of energy igniting and arcing. Electric impulses fly across from me to him, from him to me. This was a special event. Another astral adventure that was meaningful, memorable and spiritual.

The globe of creation that we shared within this astral event was not just a motivation to create the beautiful mandala of pulsating energy waves, it was symbolic of our relationship. Together Michael and I opened many doors for our students and clients. We knew we were together to create a better world, one person at a time. So it was appropriate that we would create a mandala, which is the Sanskrit word for Universe. We were altering the Universe. Our Universe and the Universe of those whose lives we would touch.

Once our energetic bodies connected within the astral planes, we were bonded on a frequency that was beyond anything that could happen on earth. Ecstasy, pure, unadulterated astral sex. More than physical love. Sex that is so pure and so complete, created by God without man's interpretation or morphing perceptions of the concept. The sex that God meant it to be on a higher plane than the physical. A deeply spiritual experience.

As I checked in with my physical body I felt that energy had permeated the physical and I was wet. I was having intense sexual feelings on the physical planes. As I put much focus back on the experience in the astral temple I realized we had taken on the cloak of Divinity, we became the personas of God and Goddess ... representations of the true male and female aspects of God making love and manifesting creation energy. The energy intensified to the highest level possible and climaxed with an explosion of energy that could have ended wars. This energy could have created world peace and healed all disease.

Michael's Journal Entry,
January 3, 2003

I woke from sleep refreshed just about 4:00 a.m. and wanting to go to the astral site which my partner and I set up for our Astral Encounters. Sleeping on my stomach with my arms wrapped around my pillow as if I am holding Mother Earth in my arms, I rolled onto my back and dropped back into an alpha state with the intention of going to our Astral Sanctuary. Within moments I (my soul and my consciousness) are at the entrance and I step (float) inside. I arrive and there are gigantic Gothic doors on the outside like twelfth-century church doors which are several stories high made of old wood and metal. I enter and immediately experience the spiritual essence of my partner, which is filling the room. She has been here, for I can feel her presence. She has been decorating again. She placed a bed within the space. It is made of crystals of different colors with light shining up through them. The bed is on the floor with hundreds of crystals arranged to cover an area of ten feet long by four feet wide. Interesting. I know this is her signature that I sense and that she has set this colorful and energetic display in place.

I have the sense that I could tap into her senses, with this much of her essence in the room, so I slowly tune into her feelings of smell, sight, hearing, touch, emotions and many others that are not defined in earth terms. One at a time, I spend fifteen to twenty minutes immersed in each of her values. As I place myself in her essence, I can see as she sees, smell as she smells, feel as she feels, etc. After experiencing each sense, I move to the next and spend fifteen to twenty minutes totally engulfed, surrounded and within her views and feelings. This is the best experiential disclosure of herself to me that I have ever experienced. I move around the room and tap into her feelings of love. I feel her love for me. I smell a rose that she has left for me at the site. A memory, a flavor, an aroma which captures my sense of smell and I stay with that aspect of her again for fifteen to twenty minutes. I roam around and in each corner of the space I am allowed to sample her thoughts about us. My consciousness drifts back to my physical body and I can feel her (physical) hand in my hand, as if she were here with my physical hand on hers. Then I drift back into our sanctuary. After a while I bump into something like the edge of the room and it startles or shakes me. I had been floating around, losing all track of time and space. All of a sudden I see her floating in the air. She has made herself visible by changing her vibration. She has been there all along as I was experiencing and exploring her. She is a beautiful being radiating a white gown made of glowing gold-white light. It clothed her as a dress streaming down from her neck - a body of light. This was her astral body.

I approached her from about ten feet away and we exchanged our feelings of love for one another. Then we approached each other and our souls merged gently and softly. As our energies mix she feels the love I have for her and I feel the love she has for me. She says in a soft whisper over and over again, "Michael, I love you." This sound, like no sound on earth, vibrated throughout my entire being; my soul and my physical body. We touch astral lips and as they merge with each other a burst of glitter in multiple colors is airborne in our midst. I chant back, "Luna, I love you." And the vibrations caress our beings in gentle waves.

This wonderful encounter is interrupted by my alarm that goes off at 6:00 a.m.. I thought I had been out of body for just a few minutes; two hours had gone by. There is so much more that happened that earth words cannot explain. I wanted to turn off the alarm and retreat to the sanctuary once more.

Luna's Journal Entry
January 3, 2003 Predawn
I go into our sacred space with a Vogel-cut crystal on my solar plexus.

I see Michael at the far side of our sanctuary, we lock eyes and giggle. We exchange our secret hand gesture, showing golden hearts that radiate out from our palm chakras. This signature signal has become a joke for us as we now feel so comfortable going to our astral sanctuary. It is now more of our secret way to say hello to each other. Then we change it up and we try to read each other's minds, changing the heart to an om symbol or a fleur de lis or something else that we try to both manifest at the same time by communicating telepathically. It is a fun astral game.

As we enter our space which resembles a Gothic church, the energy shifts immediately. This has become a place of focused intent and much energy has accumulated. It is a spiritual place above all else. Our astral energy bodies shape shift and change colors subtly as a form of communication. This has become a norm for us. We have been traveling here for a few months now and the color changes are a creative way to express our happiness to see each other.

We both appear to be more focused and centered than ever before. Our existences are evolving spiritually. The chaotic energy that appeared within the sanctuary the first few times and the excitement of the unknown has shifted to a feeling of "we are here to accomplish great things." We are now beings who are embracing the spiritual light and energy more and more each and every time we meet here. There are times that I feel our sanctuary has become a stage on which we perform for the Highest of the

High. We are both there by choice and the gratification and ecstasy that we feel from being there is beyond words. On top of all of that, we are here for the greater good. We are here to do the work of the Divine. I feel that this meeting has greater importance than ever before.

Making our approach, our astral bodies touch into each other. As we touch in, there are more color changes that take place and swirl through our astral energetic masses. This is a sexual and sensual merging that is only a small part of what is taking place. There is an energy exchange of intimate knowledge, a merging which creates a vibrational change within us. It also emits vibrations extending out from us to fill our sacred space with light that is on the orange side of golden light; a polished copper glow. A vibrant illumination of everything within the space. As this happens, a sound of ommmmmm extends out from us. A peaceful, fulfilling sound vibration on a cellular level. However, this can't be because we are out of body, we do not have our cells with us! On a soul level we understand that the om sound was cued, or set off by our etheric bodies "touching in" and that the sound entered our crowns and flowed into us with spiritual knowledge and connection to God.

Michael's and my essences are merging and that is triggering the Divine essence to flow into us with the om sound. So the merging consists of the Divine energy, Michael and myself, all three of us, merging together. The ecstatic feeling is indescribable. It is a fulfillment of a yearning that has always existed within me. It is a completion of my soul; a return to One-ness. It is satisfaction that is beyond words after a quest through many lifetimes for fulfillment on all levels of existence. The missing link put into place. This is a profound experience of becoming One with the Divine and experiencing it with another human spirit. If you can imagine becoming one with the Divine and the Divine becoming One with you and at the same time, and you are having that same experience with the one you love on the earth plane, that is the best way I can describe it. The energy exchange is beyond words. This is a loving experience that is very deep and spiritual. Ecstasy of all ecstasies.

Then just as the feeling of fulfillment is all encompassing, it pulls away. Our astral bodies retreat from each other slightly as the Divine energy rises up and out of us. There is a moment of stillness and silence. The gap between breaths. All is quiet. Then once again, another ecstatic moment, full integration of our energies with the Divine. The om sound and vibrations in copper colors wave outward from us.

As our energies mix and swirl, the knowledge is transferred on a deeply spiritual level. Retreat, silence and integration..... another wave of energy and knowledge exchange. This pattern is repeated many times. It is a slow and deliberate intercourse between me, my lover and the Divine. Oh my goodness... as I write, I think, "Who would ever believe that the Divine would show up for intercourse with human astral bodies, but in *reality, isn't that what our spirits truly are? God energy... life energy... the energy of the Creator? It starts to sink in that this is truly a profound event.*

Now as Michael and I merge our energies more and more deeply into each other, the Holy energy once again rises above us. As we are deeply engrossed in each other, we feel "raindrops" of Divine energy coming down to us. It is similar to making love in the rain but each turquoise raindrop comes down into the area of our astral bodies that have merged. Each drop penetrates our astral bodies and then dissipates. Each drop contains Divine knowledge and it merges with us according to which one of us needs that particular bit of information. We can see the turquoise color find its place within us as it merges with our connected astral bodies. The purpose of the knowledge that we are being "fed" is to help us to carry out our part of the Divine plan. This gentle rain continues until we both feel full of joy and love.

With my knowledge of the Near Death Experience and Michael's knowledge from his out-of-body experience while in a coma, the two of us expanded our knowledge and taught each other about life beyond the physical. With God's guidance our relationship expanded into one that was otherworldly.

Michael's Journal Entry
January 7, 2003

I attempt to enter the sanctuary at 5:30 a.m. I arrive at the Gothic doors and enter the space. I find my partner's essence, but she is absent. I immediately see two wooden structures in the middle of the room. I focus upon them and learn that they are two beds, like tanning beds or more like individual chambers, like wooden hot rooms, but no heat. I am given the sound of the crystal singing bowls and shown that they are chambers to project further into the outer edge of the Universe. They are meant to be used by my partner and myself to project out even further. They are piped with the sounds of the singing bowls much like the Monroe Institute's deprivation chamber in which people use hemi-sync tapes to project out of body. But when we are in our sanctuary we are already out of body. The wooden chambers are for Luna and me to enter once we arrive at our sanctuary to go even further into the unseen world, to learn to explore and bring back knowledge. They are a gift from our spirit helpers. The wooden beds are of simple construction. Just a place to recline, closed off from the influences of the physical world and into which the vibrational soundtrack of the bowls passes through one's body. It is an off-earth chamber from which we move deeper into the discoveries of the Divine. Mmmmmmm.... I can't wait to try it. Then I was woken up with the alarm at 6:00 a.m.

After more than four months of meeting in the astral planes, we finally left our spouses and combined our living arrangements on January 14, 2003. All of the astral sanctuary experiences were just a prelude to what our lives would become over the next twelve years.

Having an astral romance is something that could enrich many lives. This could be one way of evolving our society to a new level. Raising the consciousness from the chaos and materialism of the physical world, bringing the souls of the participants closer to God, feeling true unconditional love and One-ness with the Divine – this is an opportunity for spiritual growth. Leaving the Earth's influences behind, a spirit can experience the true knowledge of who they are and what their life's purpose is.

I would like to add that because Michael and I respected each other's soul signature boundaries we were able to develop a relationship that was connected to God. Michael and I were consenting astral bodies and respected and honored each other within the process of merging our soul signatures. If you decide to travel within the astral planes, you are in an altered brain wave state, much like hypnosis. This makes you vulnerable to mind control and manipulation. If you are to attempt anything like this it is best if you have a teacher who can teach you about setting up protection and also about the Karma of invading the energy of another without permission.

Michael and I met at our astral location often until we could be together in the physical planes.

Michael continued to open doors for me, revealing what life in the astral planes was all about. He was a spirit guide of sorts who fell out of the sky and into my life. The two of us expanded our knowledge and taught each other and with God's guidance our relationship expanded into one that was otherworldly.

We later used astral travel to do remote healings, Remote Viewings and to effect matter remotely realizing that so much could be accomplished in such a short time in the astral planes. Manifestation takes only a thought to make a change take place. This concept has held true for so many applications such as remote healings.

Michael's Dream
January 6, 2003

Luna and I are holding an infant. The infant begins to speak to us in word groups that far exceed any childlike understanding, in the mature voice of an adult. I get the sense that this is the Divine speaking to us. "You have given birth to an idea that will help many. It is your responsibility to grow this new inspirational thought form and to deliver it to the human population. You are to present this concept to humanity against all odds so they can benefit from its value. It will advance humankind."

Michael and I experienced many past lives together. We reconnected and in doing so we became each other's teachers and students. We focused on life on the other side of the veil. Our astral romance was a beautiful experience but the byproduct was even more important. With all of our time out of our bodies, we gained a closeness to God that I had never known was possible. It was similar to re-living my Near Death Experience. It was a One-ness that I have not been able to achieve on the physical earthly plane.

How do you think you could incorporate the process of meeting your loved one in the astral planes? If one of you travels for business or is bedridden or has physical limitations, the process of astral romance could open doors for you. It could expand your relationship to a higher level of one that incorporates the energy of the Creator. This is your Divine right to accomplish what God meant for you to experience. You can have experiences similar to those that Michael and I had. It is a matter of you and your partner being on the same page. Michael and I were not special beings; this is an experience that you can add to your relationships now. We were able to experience it because we were motivated and we felt we were destined to be together. You can add this heavenly dimension to your life.

Fourteen
Zapped, Tapped, and Trapped

"[Saint Anthony] said, in his solitude, he sometimes encountered devils who looked like angels, and other times he found angels who looked like devils. When asked how he could tell the difference, the saint said that you can only tell which is which by the way you feel after the creature has left your company."
"Eat, Pray, Love" by Elizabeth Gilbert.

The gift of clairvoyance was a Divine gift. Trusting those messages and knowing that yes, they do come directly from God – that is another Divine gift. However there have been side effects. There have been some challenges, as a result of a shift of energy, that have made it more difficult to live in the three-dimensional world, saturated by electronics.

One challenge has been an intense energy coming from my hands that did not used to be there, especially when there is emotion involved. One day I was upset with Michael. Anger was raging inside me and I broke the thermostat, the microwave and the computer just by touching them. That was an expensive day!

There are times when the TV will come on just because I walk into the room, as if I am a human remote control. I also have accidentally magnetized silverware so it sticks together. One time at dinner with a scientist friend of ours, I picked up my fork and it was stuck to the knife, both coming off the table together. My scientist friend looked at me with eyes wide and said "How did you do that?" I laughed as he tried to get his silverware to stick together with magnetic energy. My response to him was, "I have no idea. It just happens sometimes."

Going to the grocery store has become a challenge as I routinely lock up the cash register computer just by being near it. The typical response from the cashier that is trying to help me: "That's never happened before!"

The worse experience was when Michael was in the emergency room during his last month of occupying his physical body. I was sitting in the room with him and the nurse was trying to take his vitals. The nurse exhaled in frustration and said, "Well, that's never happened before!" Michael and I locked eyes with a little smile. "Luna, please go out in the hallway," Michael suggested to me in a controlled but whimsical tone. Of course, as soon as I left the room the vitals machine started working again.

Even now, sitting here typing, the computer changes fonts, erases what I am writing and the cursor jumps around the screen seemingly at will but I know better than to blame the computer. I just need to ground my excess energies.

I have found that this challenge manifests mostly when my emotions are intensified. I attribute it to the amount of time that I spend in the astral planes. I think the out-of-body time alters the frequency of my spirit body and when I am in my physical body, the energy that is being emitted alters the frequency of electronics and creates a blockage of energy flow.

Being clairvoyant leaves me exposed to communications and emotions that most people are protected from. If I see someone who walks with a limp, I not only sense that they have a back or knee injury, I actually feel their pain. I probably also experience the fall down the stairs or spousal abuse or skiing accident that caused their injury. I had to become adept at manifesting protection around myself in these cases. Typically I am initially caught off guard when, for example, I am sitting at a stop light and watching someone traverse a crosswalk with difficulty. Then I feel the ache in the pit of my stomach as information about the disability begins to enter my energetic field. As soon as that feeling hits, I put up protection around me.

I know that when I visit a friend in the hospital or especially hospice that I need to put up protection. With all of the grief and worry and fear that takes place in those locations, there is a chaotic energy that is stored at the site. This energy is something that I have become adept at picking up due to all of the Remote Viewing work I have done for the government as well as police departments. Being able to tap into the stored energy at a location is an important tool for that work.

One time I was totally caught off guard at a presentation by John Edwards, psychic medium. As I scurried up the stairs to the building, I was smothered with a tsunami of emotions. I felt faint as my knees buckled beneath me. I was not sure what was happening until I realized that there were many people that came to this event hoping that John Edwards would help them connect with their deceased loved ones. Memories of suicides, auto accidents and other tragic deaths had imprinted a dark cloud of energy that hung in the space surrounding the building. Once I had clarity of what was happening, I was able to ground out the dark energy and put up a blanket of protection around me.

Another change that I experienced was that openness to the other side is not always positive. There are many layers of energy within the astral planes. Disincarnated beings exist in some of the lower realms. These can be beings who died so suddenly that they are confused and have not moved into the light. They can be spirits that died violently or had severe addictions prior to dropping their physical bodies.

Some disincarnated beings can become "attachments." These are spirits that attach to people who have energetic imbalances and can cause mental illness or addictions. I have encountered the attachments many times when working with clients to resolve alcoholism, drug addiction and mental illness. I perceive the attachments to be hanging around in the person's energy field, usually around the right shoulder. When I am entering into a healing of that sort, I put up a lot of protection. Spirits have different frequencies and if they are enlightened beings when they leave their bodies, they will raise up to the highest of realms and become one with God. Low-level spirits will sometimes be so low to earth that they don't even realize they have died. Typically these spirits will attach to someone whose energy is not balanced for some reason. Spirits are attracted to beings with similar frequencies within the astral planes. In addition to putting up protection when working these healings, I make sure that I am balanced and centered and protected prior to leaving my body to accomplish the work.

Early on, I was not aware that I was open to attachments. Typically I am a very positive person, full of loving energy that radiates outward from my heart. During a time when my life was chaotic and in a state of upheaval, I was in a very low-level frequency. I was consuming a lot of alcohol. I had chosen to move into an apartment that was near Fort Logan Cemetery and Fort Logan Mental Health Hospital, and for some strange reason I was driven to purchase a book about dark energies. All of this was out of context for me. In retrospect I think that a dark spirit took control of my physical body to lead me to where he wanted me to be. The book was fiction and it dealt with dark sex and couples taking S&M bondage to the limits. They were using "safe words" to tell their partners that they were crossing over the line and taking things too far. The fact that I was reading that book shows what a dark place I was in in my life. I was sitting in a chair reading the book and suddenly I felt surrounded by a very dark disincarnated being. Feeling overcome with the evilness of the entity, I got up and threw the book away. I had a lot of red wine that night. I was not myself. I dragged myself to bed and just as I was drifting off to sleep, I felt something flip me onto my back, hold my hands down over my head and rape me repeatedly. My energetic field was being invaded by a disincarnated spirit that felt mentally ill, aggressive and dark. I consider this spirit to be truly evil. I tried to scream but my throat was so constricted that I produced no sound. I was experiencing pure terror. I am not sure how long I endured the attack. And I am not sure why I had to experience this terrible violation.

Once released, I pulled my mattress off my bed and got it into my living room and put it on the floor. I closed the bedroom door behind me. Afraid to go to sleep, I said prayers of protection the rest of the night. The next morning, in the safety of the daylight, and surrounding myself with the highest frequency of protective light, I went back into that room only once to gather up everything I needed until I moved out of that apartment one month later, never to go back. In fact, I even avoided driving anywhere near that apartment building again.

This was an unforgettable lesson that I would hold dear to me for the rest of my life. I am now very conscious of the type of energies to which I expose myself, putting up protection whenever needed. And when I teach my students to leave their bodies, I follow a protocol which takes them only to the highest of realms.

Fifteen
Miracles From the Other Side

"Trust in me and your prayer shall be answered."
Sai Baba

After Michael was diagnosed with Non-Hodgkin's Lymphoma, we both became Reiki Master Teachers. He made the decision to follow traditional healing methods as well as alternative ones. He hit the disease with everything that was available. He followed a traditional protocol of chemotherapy and radiation, as well as hands-on healing, visualizations, dietary changes, meditation and many other modalities. Michael was focused on beating the odds. The doctor told him that after the chemotherapy and radiation regime, lymphoma would most likely re-manifest within three years and unless medical science had advanced by then, there would be nothing that we could do. It would be the end of his life. Thinking that we had three years to turn things around, together we made positive changes in our lives. We protected ourselves from any negativity by no longer watching or reading the news, and discontinuing interactions with any people who carried negative or pessimistic energies. Together we were full of hope and optimism certain that we could beat the odds.

Then the rug got pulled out from under us.

Eight months after finishing his last set of radiation treatments, a new tumor emerged on Michael's ankle. The doctors scheduled him for more radiation. Feeling used up and full of frustration, we left for an extended trip to Mexico and planned to return to the United States the day before a new regime of radiation would begin.

During our time in Mexico, we sprawled on the beach, taking in the energy of the ocean waves. We combined the energy of the Caribbean off the coast of Cozumel with Reiki energy and directed it to the area on his ankle that had the issue. Right before we left on our trip we had completed a level two workshop at the Shambala Mountain Center in Colorado with Dr. Joe Dispenza, author of "Evolve Your Brain", "Breaking the Habit of Being Yourself" and "You Are The Placebo". The focus of Dr. Dispenza's work included a shift of behavioral and thought patterns creating chemical reactions which in turn connect new synapses in the brain. As Reiki Masters we understood that by changing the emotional patterns, physical changes could take place. We used our newest Dispenza tools and also we met a Mexican shaman named Gambino who performed healing on Michael. The entire trip, we focused on healing.

Michael would later give impromptu presentations at Dr. Dispenza's workshops stating that he realized that he had a "marble of resentment" rolling around in his head that had manifested physically as the cancerous tumor on his ankle. The resentment grew from unresolved feelings involving his clandestine undercover work funded by Ross Perot, finding and documenting the capture and imprisonment of American POW's and MIA's. After Michael reported his findings to the United States government, the men were never rescued. This was a hurtful and frustrating truth that Michael had to put to rest in his mind. Michael's interpretation of the miraculous healing was that he grabbed ahold of the "marble of resentment" and threw it into the ocean, and never looked back. Whatever it was that he did, it worked! Possibly it was the combination of all the changes he made.

When we returned home, Michael got in the shower and the tumor fell off his ankle. We were elated. If we had any doubts about the power of alternative healing before this, we were now 100% on board. Michael called the radiologist's office and told them he should probably cancel his appointment because the tumor was gone. Of course the doctor's office was skeptical and asked him to come in anyway. They had taken photos of the tumor before we left for our trip and tattooed him to line up the radiation equipment. They had good documentation of what the tumor used to look like. No one could believe that the tumor could fall off. Of course they wanted to see where the tumor no longer existed. When Michael went into the radiation office, the doctor could not get near him. The nurses were all gathered around him "oohing" and "ahhhing." Michael did agree to continue with the planned radiation treatments as a precautionary measure because the doctors were concerned that there could be residual cancer hiding underneath the skin.

We know that cancer tumors do not typically fall off. This miraculous healing motivated us to continue to do more healings for others. We moved forward as healers without self-imposed obstacles. We felt that if God was willing, we could heal anyone. You also have these abilities. Staying positive and full of hope is the path to coherence, and using the energy of miracles from God.

Another impressive remote healing that Michael and I facilitated together involved Teresa Sterns in Minnesota. Michael and I did a series of six remote sessions with her to dissolve a tumor.

As I approached Teresa's spirit for healing, I followed a protocol that was similar each time.

Here are my notes from a typical healing session with Teresa.

I entered trance and approached Teresa's soul signature asking for approval for healing. After finding out that she was open to healing energies, I scanned her major chakras. I cleared dark energy from any blockages I found. (Typically I have specifics about what I sense and what needs to be cleared but due to client confidentiality I am not putting the details here.) I cleared each blockage and asked God to heal any area that needed it. I removed fear, anxiety, worry and any other negative emotion that could create an obstacle for healing. I sent love and light to her energy body. I visualized her as whole and complete. I saw her as clear and at One with the Divine... pure golden light energy that no darkness can penetrate. I then sealed in the Reiki energy so it will continue to facilitate and perpetuate her healing process.

This is a condensed version of one of the healing sessions that I did for Teresa. A typical session lasts for one hour. Michael and I worked side by side doing the healings simultaneously. Of course, Teresa followed many other protocols to facilitate her healing. Michael and I were honored to be part of her rebirth process as a healthy woman.

Review of Healing
Written by Teresa Sterns

Late in 2013 and early 2014 I participated with Luna and Michael Van Atta in healing sessions that brought amazing love energy into my life. I had been diagnosed with stage 3 endometrial cancer and after surgery there remained one tumor that was missed. With no chemo or radiation, but much love, great nutrition, Reiki and infrared therapy, the tumor disappeared and I have been healthy since. I found the work with Luna and Michael pivotal. At one point they said, "Have you asked for a miracle?" "No," I said. "Well ask!" they said. So I did! And the day before my scan, I awoke with a knowing. A voice, clear as a bell said to me,

"Teresa, you are healed." I jumped out of bed with a huge smile on my face and tears in my eyes, "I am healed," I said. Three days later, the PetCT scan results came back. "No evidence of metastatic disease." I have had four scans since then, all with the same result. I so value having learned to call upon the love/God energy (that is everything in and around us) to help me. My gratitude to Luna and Michael is huge.

As this book nears publication I found out that Teresa is coming for a visit. Although I feel that I already know her in the astral world, this will be the first time that I actually meet her in person. I am truly looking forward to this meeting with her in the physical plane.

As of this writing Teresa remains cancer-free and living her miracle.

Edgar Cayce is involved in many of my healings as he has chosen to work with me from the other side of the veil. I have deep gratitude that such a profound healer is on my team. One night in 2004, Mr. Cayce came to me in a dream. I had a severe respiratory infection at the time and I was very close to being admitted to the hospital. In the dream, Edgar showed me a copper pyramid with a Vogel-cut crystal hanging from it that I needed to have over my bed for healing. This dream spoke to me on a very deep level since I had been working with Vogel-cut crystals in my healing work as well as etheric communications. (I will explain more about this special type of crystal later.) I felt I received a healing from him that night, as that was a turning point of the respiratory issue moving away and my health returning.

He also provided me with a lesson within the dream. He told me that once I have healed from the infection that I should go into the astral planes and manifest a temple. I was to infuse the temple with my own healthy energy so that anytime I became ill I could go to that location and get a "transfusion" of my own optimum energy. This was much like giving blood before an operation so that you get your own blood if you need a transfusion. Edgar explained to me that by doing this, the healing energy from my own soul signature would resonate best for my own personal healing.

The concept of the astral location that Edgar Cayce downloaded into my brain during sleep became a tool that I have used in many astral applications for distance healing as well as in teaching my students to meet with their deceased loved ones.

I told Michael about the dream and that Edgar had directed me to place the copper pyramid over the bed. Michael purchased copper tubing in an effort to complete the task. However, he was not a handy person and the tubing never did manifest into a pyramid.

Months later, we ran into a client – who I will call Craig – in the parking lot of a meeting for a group called Paranormal Research Society. Michael and I had done many remote healing sessions for this gentleman who had a serious issue. He had been diagnosed with cancer of the tongue and lower jaw and traditional medical doctors had removed both to the point of taking away his ability to speak. After several remote healing sessions, the gentleman's tongue grew back to the point he was able to speak again.

Running into him in the parking lot was a surprise. We had not seen him or interacted with him for about six months. He rushed up to us with a big smile. *"I am so glad to see you both! I have made something for you, a gift of appreciation and I have been carrying it around with me in the back of my truck."*

We walked over to the truck with him and there was a large copper pyramid, approximately 36" square at the base, with a loop at the top for hanging. Somehow Edgar Cayce had planted the information in Craig's brain to build this beautiful pyramid. I was so grateful that Edgar was working behind the scenes to make sure that I got my pyramid and what a wonderful way to receive it, as a gratitude gift from someone whose life had changed due to our work with him.

We took the pyramid home, placed a Vogel-cut quartz crystal in the center and hung it over the bed in our healing room to use with our clients. Thank you Edgar Cayce and Craig, you are the teachers of those of us who are called to be healers. Teachers come in all forms – spirit guides as well as clients.

Each time we were successful in a miraculous healing, it reinforced our abilities and helped us to not impose doubts when asked for a new healing challenge. We learned not to restrict our thoughts of any outcome, always visualizing the client as healed and whole. We were witnessing miracles of God working through us that were extraordinary.

One day the phone rang and it was a medical doctor whom we met when he became a Remote Viewing student of ours. I will call him Dr. Levit. He called from Delaware to say he had lost his eyesight due to diabetic retinopathy. We listened to him as his wife was driving him to a specialist. He was in a panic. He had pictures with him of the bleeding in the back of his eye that was causing the blindness. Michael and I dropped everything and immediately went to work on him remotely.

Testimonial of Restored Eyesight

"I lost my eyesight due to diabetic retinopathy. I am so grateful that I called you while I was on my way to the eye specialist. You immediately sat down and did a distance healing on me. Thirty minutes later, walking into the eye specialist's office, with diagnostic photos in hand. The specialist could not find any bleeding and did not even think that the photos indicating the bleeding could have been mine. I was healed and my eyesight was restored. I am forever grateful to you."

In one distance-healing session we were able to restore his eyesight. We knew that it was truly not us doing the healing work. It was God working through us. As Reiki Masters, we only become clear vessels for God to work through us.

One of the most interesting cases I ever worked was for Esther in Boulder, Colorado. Esther was diagnosed with Dissociative Identity Disorder. Esther was a unique person and she had spent many years becoming comfortable with her multiple personalities instead of trying to eliminate or suppress them. She had integrated them all into her life and was comfortable with where she was in the process. Each of them were taking turns using her physical body so that she could navigate her way through the 3-D world. She called upon the talents of each of her personalities to help her in whatever scenario life threw at her.

Her current health issue had to do with a tumor on her ovary. Esther was scheduled for surgery and called us to help shrink the tumor. Before she hung up she made us promise to not try to remove any of the personalities that had become like family members to her. So this would be an interesting and challenging process of remotely effecting the tumor without disturbing the personalities. We would be dissolving the tumor from a distance.

I went into an altered brain state and sent my spirit to her spirit to ask permission for the healing. I was given a yes for the tumor and a no for the multiple personalities. This is the same thing that Esther had said verbally when requesting the healing. I surrounded our spirits with golden light of protection for the healing. I have found that most times when accessing multiple personalities in the astral planes, they show up as attachments. I wanted to be sure to protect myself from any attachments that might disconnect from her and latch onto me.

However, once I connected to Esther's spirit I found out that her personalities were not attachments or entities. I "saw" Esther's energy signature with an umbilical cord- like feature extending way out from her solar plexus. "Skewered" on the umbilical cord through the solar plexus areas were separate personalities with spaces in between. Each of the personalities was represented in this vision. This was something I had never seen before. Typically I see entities or attachments hanging around the shoulders of a person, usually on the right side. Esther's personalities were like living beings attached to this umbilical cord. All but one looked human, that one looked almost like a dinosaur.

Michael and I worked on shrinking the tumor and visualized it as nonexistent. After the healing I drew a diagram of the personalities and how I had perceived them. When I reported this to Esther, she had a wonderful comfort level with all of it. She requested the drawing that I made of the entities extending out from her soul signature. I was happy to provide it, hoping that it would further her full integration of the different personalities.

The tumor was still present when she reported for surgery the following week. However, the doctors told Esther after the operation that it had decreased to half the size of the original that was shown on the diagnostic tests. Perhaps if we had more time...

Another case: When we worked on Nathan in Boulder, Colorado we knew we were only going to have one shot at helping him heal. His mother called us and asked for healing for her twelve-year-old son. He had fallen off his bicycle and was found unconscious, lying on the pavement. The head injury left him with severe head pain and dizziness and he was unable to go to school or use the motor skills needed to walk.

When we arrived at the home, there was tension in the air. The father was obviously not on board with the healing. He left in a huff and the mother asked us to continue. Most importantly, we needed to know if the son wanted healing. We would never attempt a healing without permission of the person receiving it. Nathan said yes, he wanted us to continue. We knew that we would not be asked back, due to the friction between the mother and father, so after our healing session we gave Nathan a Reiki attunement and taught him how to work on himself. He immediately put his hands to his head and continued the treatment that we had initiated. It is was not typical for us to attune someone to Reiki without complete training but in this case it was the right thing to do. Nathan was wise beyond his years – he was twelve-years-old going on twenty-five. He was motivated to heal and he had no self-imposed obstacles around succeeding.

Thank You Letter From Nathan

Mike and Luna are both heroes in my life. They helped me recover from a concussion and vestibular issue and I am thankful for their healing and prayers. They really helped me out in a hard time. Before they did their healing, I had been out of school for more than a month and had difficulty with eye tracking but most of all I had really bad dizziness and headaches. When they came over to our house, I was a little nervous but when I felt their works spreading throughout my body, I knew they were doing good. A few days after they left, I took my first steps unassisted, my headaches decreased and a few weeks later, I began to track with my eyes better. I am now fully recovered thanks to Mike and Luna and I don't know how I would have been now without them. Thank you. N.K. Boulder, Colorado

There are many, many more healings that God accomplished through our hands. And the miracles continue now with Michael on the other side as one of my guides. I am eternally grateful for all of the healings that happen through me. I am living my life's purpose.

How can you incorporate miracles into your own life? Stay positive and be receptive to God energy. That is where all miracles begin. God is the ultimate healer and you have the ability to tap into that energy of Creation.

Sixteen
Passing the Test

*"In life you'll realize there is a purpose for everyone you
meet. Some will test you, some will teach you,
and some will use you. But most importantly,
some will bring out the best in you."*
Ditaba Daniel

As our lives progressed Michael and I began
teaching workshops together on Remote Viewing
and astral travel. In 2010 we were teaching a
class at The Caritas Spiritist Center in Boulder,
Colorado and Jean Torkelson, spiritual reporter
for the local newspaper, the Boulder Daily
Camera, arrived to observe and interview us.

We felt some pressure as we were exercising
our left brains while teaching to stay organized
and then Ms. Torkelson wanted us to Remote
View something to "prove" ourselves. Remote
Viewing and teaching involve opposite sides of
the brain. These two sides of the brain typically
do not resonate with each other. So teaching
Remote Viewing is a challenge in itself. Being
observed, judged and interviewed for a
newspaper at the same time intensifies that

challenge. It can create a great amount of pressure, especially in front of our students. And what Remote Viewer wants to have a bad day when they can't connect to the target and have that published in the newspaper?

Declining the test would have only undermined our credibility, so we agreed to be tested. She was, after all, a newspaper reporter and refusing to submit to the trial, would have been read as a failure. If someone asks you to prove yourself it can be difficult to stay out of body and focus on the target because it brings in self-doubt. Doubt is all about the ego according to my experiences, astral travel and Remote Viewing are spirit based and the two do not normally go together. Jean decided she would test us and the pressure was on. She left the room with one of the wooden boxes and put an item in it. She returned to the room and asked us to Remote View it. I immediately started to get hits and aspects of the target. I wrote down my hits. When our viewings were completed, Michael hung back, not offering anything and deferred to me.

I decided to just blurt out the aspects that I perceived:

Black, hard surface, plastic, rectangular with a round area that has small holes that are positioned in lines, and an energy signature that felt like a battery but weaker.

Jean was quite amazed as she pulled her small handheld black rectangular recorder from the box and stated that her batteries were almost dead. So much for skeptics!

Jean Torkelson wrote a very nice piece about us in her column in the Boulder Daily Camera.

Seventeen

Missing Furry Ones and Other Things

"In my experience even inanimate objects have a will of their own, and they won't be found until they want to be, until they're good and ready."
Menna van Praag

Michael and I worked many cases for many people. Remote Viewing is an imperfect system and there are never any promises that your information is going to be 100% spot on. This is why there are usually several people working the same target.

Reviewing missing pet targets, I remember one in particular that stood out – a missing dog that needed medication. The small dog had run out through an open gate and quickly vanished. The owner was distraught and like so many pet owners, her dog was like a child to her. The dog would not survive long without its medication. As soon as we got the call we immediately went to work. We received information in our viewings that the dog was being held by an elderly woman as a companion for her granddaughter. The details came in to us as messages from our guides and angels. That is typically the way that we would receive the information. We perceived the dog as being treated well although it was not getting its much-needed medication. We also were downloaded information that it was important for the owner go to nearby veterinary offices with flyers showing the dog's picture and her phone number.

The grandmother seemed resistant to giving up the dog as she and her granddaughter were becoming attached to it. The dog had been missing for a week. I focused on the location of the dog. I saw the street name on a green street sign with white lettering: Trenton Ave. I saw which house the dog was in, a blue-gray tri-level with low-lying juniper bushes in the front yard. Now the decision point...do I give this information to the owner of the dog? Do I go to the home and confront the grandmother? I came out of trance and talked with Michael. "What is the best way to handle this?" As always, Michael was one step ahead of me.

"It's going to be okay," he said with a smile.

"Why," I asked, *"what did you do?"*

"I talked to the soul of the grandmother." His grin growing wider. *"I asked her to do the right thing."*

One hour later we received a call from Cindy, the doggie mommy. She gushed, *"I just picked up Fluffy! A lady turned her into the veterinary office down the street from me and she is doing okay. I* have her back on her medications and I am so happy and so grateful for all of the work you both did to help her get back home."

The grandmother had mentioned to the vet that her granddaughter was already attached to the dog but she decided to "do the right thing."

Another happy ending!

Sending someone the thought form to do the right thing is something you can incorporate into your life. It is a matter of clarifying your intention and using emotion to broadcast it into the energy field. This is not about mind control. It is about working in coherence with the greater good. It is important to incorporate good ethical decisions within this process, always focusing on the best possible outcome without compromising someone's free will.

Sporadically we would be contacted to find all types of items. Missing jewelry or keys were common targets. I received a call from a friend one day stating that she was looking for her wooden animal sculptures that she had purchased in Oaxaca, Mexico. She had looked everywhere and was unable to find them. I had never been to her house before, but of course in the world of Remote Viewing that does not matter. I obtained her permission to Remote View her house, and accessed the target.

Viewing of Friend's
Missing Sculptures
"I sent my astral double to your home and then I entered your front door and went down a

hallway, then opened a door on my right and went down the stairs into the basement. There are built-in shelves under your stairs, or maybe a bookcase. I saw the items on one of the two lowest shelves wrapped in tissue paper or cloth."

The friend was amazed that not only did I have the layout of her home correct but also the location of the missing items.

Eighteen
Special Delivery

"The key to spiritual enlightenment, joy on earth, connection to the laws of nature, optimum health, the meaning of life and peace of mind all stems from embracing the relationship we have with the Divine. It can all be condensed down to five words: 'perfect love and perfect trust.' Perfect love speaks of knowing the Divine on a personal level. Perfect trust means putting the intention out into the Universe and then allowing that intention or wish to unfold in whatever manner is correct within the context of the Divine plan."
Michael Van Atta, January 4, 2003

While working a missing-person case I received an email from Liz Beth's spirit. We will probably never really know how the internet and the astral planes tie in together but somehow Liz Beth was able to send me an email regarding a TASER gun that had been used in a murder case I was working on. Once I received her email regarding the TASER gun, I went back into a trance to ask my guides how this new piece of information entered into the situation. I was shown the TASER hidden under the driver's seat of an old Chevy pickup truck. This information was provided to the police department that was working on that particular case.

Working the intensely emotional murder cases with Michael and his unconditional acceptance of the messages I was receiving, bonded us on a very deep level. Here was a man that I had spent many past lives with and now we were doing this very important work. Could it be that this was why God brought us together in this lifetime? We had work to do, we had a mission of greater good that exceeded any relationship I had ever remembered experiencing in any lifetime. The love that we felt for each other within months was deep and pure and beyond anything that most people would experience. The depth of our work beyond the veil told me that I would no longer be happy working in an office as an insurance agent.

After Michael's death, he was able to use electronics to connect with me from the other side. A couple of weeks after Michael died, my cell phone started ringing. I looked at the display which said "Michael Van Atta." I panicked... my dead husband was calling me from the other side of the veil! I was so excited, confused and surprised that I pushed the decline button; something I will regret for the rest of my life. I sat down with amazement permeating my every cell of my body. I checked my cell phone display again for incoming calls and there it was: "Michael Van Atta;" the display that would have shown if he was calling me from his cell phone. Could Michael have actually figured out a way to contact me from beyond the veil through electronic frequencies? What would have happened if I had answered it? This was a new experience for me. I had traveled in the astral realms and I had many out-of-the-ordinary experiences but to get a phone call from heaven, well this was truly over the top.

I decided to take the SIM card out of Michael's phone. I am not sure why this phone call made me feel so off kilter. Possibly because I no longer had Michael Van Atta in my physical life and I wished I could have spoken with him on the phone.

It was such a goofy thing for me to decline the call. I thought no one would ever believe me. I should have welcomed a chance to talk with him and get some inside knowledge as to how he was doing and some confirmation of what I imagined his astral life to be. Four days later my phone rang again, with the "Michael Van Atta" display showing me who called. This time, I took a deep breath and answered it. "Honey? Are you there? Can you hear me?" Only silence on the other end of the phone. If Michael was indeed able to somehow tap into the phone and orchestrate a call to me, I was unfortunately unable to hear him. I called out to him a few more times just in case. "Michael? Michael? Are you calling me, hon?" Still nothing.

After a few minutes I hung up, feeling great disappointment. The only explanation I can give for this is that his voice was at a frequency I could not hear. This reminded me of the dream I had where I was trying to call Michael as he was ascending in an airplane and we were on different frequencies. Since then, I have heard of other people who have received cell phone calls from the other side of the veil. Validation that I am indeed sane! The knowledge that you are watching over me, Michael, is very comforting.

Every morning for one full year after Michael left this lifetime I called his spirit in and had a conversation with him. My communication with Michael was always clearest in the mornings. I followed his progression from leaving his body, to meeting with God, to going through a life review, and meeting with the Ascended Masters about what his next lessons would entail in future lives. At this time, Michael is still in the spirit world and has not reincarnated. His current job description involves helping people to recognize their healing gifts. He is also working on the other side to provide knowledge to scientists that are "in body" to help them figure out how to morph cancer cells into healthy ones with a focus on children who have been diagnosed with cancer.

I have also been given information from Michael that he has been instrumental in bringing me a new life partner who is so much like me I feel he is a soul mate.

Thank you Michael, for all of the good work you are doing. It gives me great comfort to know that you are watching over me from the other side of the veil.

Nineteen

A New Trilogy:
Michael, Jesus and George Carlin

*"I have as much authority as the pope,
I just don't have as many people who believe it."*
George Carlin

It seemed that I could receive clearer messages from Michael without the phone. On the day that Michael dropped his body, hospice came to pick up the physical shell. Michael's body lay on the hospice bed with a sheet over him. He had on no shirt and his underwear had been cut down the sides to allow for the nurse to insert a catheter the day before with as little disturbance as possible due to the pain he was in which broke through the fog of morphine.

In getting the body ready for transport, the hospice nurse asked me if I wanted to get some clothes for Michael to wear out the door. At first I said "No, it is just a shell, that is not really Michael, I doubt that he even cares if his body has clothes on it." Then I got a very strong statement from Michael saying "I want to wear my George

Carlin T-shirt." There he was, making me smile at such a traumatic time. As with some of the very surprising and more unusual messages that I get, I "tapped in" and thought, *Really? Am I hearing this correctly?* There was no doubt in my mind that this was a clear message from Michael, always wanting to make everyone laugh.

Then, as if he had taken me by the hand and guided me up the stairs to the dresser, I pulled out the drawer and there right on top was the t-shirt he had asked for. Interesting that it was right on top as he had not worn it for many months. It was a black t-shirt with a white caricature of George Carlin on the front. Michael purchased the shirt a few years ago when we had attended a George Carlin performance in Denver. On the back was the statement in bold letters *'Look busy, Jesus is coming'*. I burst out in laughter. My husband had just died and his sense of humor was coming forward from the other side. He made me laugh. I grabbed the shirt and a pair of khaki shorts and made my way down the stairs. He wanted to make me laugh and he wanted to make a memorable exit. And so, out the door they went, Michael, Jesus and George Carlin.

Twenty
Presents From Heaven

*"So far as I am concerned, this is evidence of my divinity.
It is not by any means an exhibition of my divinity.
For me this is a kind of calling card to convince people of
my love for them and secure their devotion in return.
Since love is formless, I do materialization as
evidence of My Love. It is merely a symbol."*
Sri Sathya Sai Baba

Coming out of a very deep mediation; at our Colorado mountain cabin. We emerged from a state of fogginess to reintegrate into the physical world. We had been in trance for forty-five minutes or more. Michael and I had done this many times before, sitting on the hardwood floor of the old 1800's cabin, away from phones, computers, and television, we were able to achieve deeply altered states of consciousness. We were traveling through the astral planes having off-earth experiences. As we both came back into our bodies, lying on the floor before us were four tiny pearls.

I had heard about apport before but thought it was something that was achieved only by enlightened beings such as Sai Baba. Apport can also be called materialization. Many people have thought it is a sleight-of-hand trick and attached to deceitful or fraudulent activities. I can tell you that Michael and I never expected this to happen. We did not go out of body with the intent to try to accomplish something so profound. We were having an afternoon that for us was normal; a little astral travel. The apported items were a present from heaven.

Over the years there would be other things that materialized or followed us back from the other side; coins from Aruba and the Netherlands, a rusty nail, a small faceted amethyst, a silver dragonfly. Each time it happened it was a gift coming through from the other side of the veil and always unexpected.

For us, apport was an unexpected and peripheral experience; the items just appeared in front of us on the floor. The first time this happened, we were amazed and a little confused. Possibly we somehow opened a portal in the fabric of the veil and the items came through. I wish I could explain it better. I do not have the answers. I have saved all of the early items in a sacred place in my healing room.

The most extraordinary apports for me were after Michael passed over. The gifts that I received from him hold a very special place in my heart. The first one appeared while we were planning his memorial service at Poco Diablo Resort, in Sedona, Arizona. We were gathered around a large table on the patio talking about him. His sisters Ann and Patty were there, as well as my very good friends Leah and Larry. We were having lunch. There was a wedding reception happening at the other end of the patio and a slow song came on. I commented that if Michael were there he would be asking me to dance. And so my sisters-in-law immediately asked me to dance with them as if Michael had come into the body of first one sister and then the other to slow-dance with me. I sobbed and sobbed, missing him so much. Then sitting back at the table, as we discussed Michael further and feeling his presence so very strongly around me I looked down in my hands and there was a bent spoon! Michael and I taught many people to bend spoons over the years. Many times we used it as a "de-tune process" at the end of teaching a Remote Viewing or astral travel class.

Now, it was as if Michael had taken over my body. He used my hands to throw the spoon into the middle of the table with a flourish just as he would have done with a "ta-da!" Everyone looked and I told them Michael placed a bent spoon in my hands from the other side.

After accumulating many bent spoons in our home over the years we realized that Michael always bent his spoon inward and I bent my spoons outward, so we could always tell who had bent which spoon. Here in my hands was an inwardly bent spoon that had aported from the other side. Bent spoons were something that had been prevalent in our relationship; it made a lot of sense that I would receive such a significant gift from Michael. It was his way of letting everyone know he was there at the table with us, listening in as we planned his memorial.

I received a couple of more gifts from Michael after he passed. The most extraordinary gift was a bear's claw. About two weeks after Michael passed away, I was in the garage getting ready to get into the car and I felt something under my foot. When I looked down there was a new gift from Michael; a bear's claw! Oh my goodness, what a wonderful gift. This gift reminded me of our home in Colorado that was on seven acres and backed up to National Forest land. There were two bears that would visit us, a black bear and a cinnamon-colored one. I had this very special gift made into a pendant. Thank you Michael, for giving me these concrete gifts to let me know that you are around me.

It is no surprise that Michael would reach out to me from the other side. He was all about communication between the spirit world and the physical world when he was in his body; why would that change now?

One day, I was sitting in the living room with the T.V. on with a friend and all of a sudden Michael's picture popped up on the screen. It was a picture that his hiking buddy Larry took when they were on a beautiful Sedona red rock trail. We burst out in laughter. What a surprise! That was Michael all right. Always trying to catch everyone off guard and make them laugh.

Many people have commented on how quickly I healed my emotional pain of losing Michael after we had been so close. My best explanation is that first of all I don't truly feel I have lost him; he is around me and with me all the time. Also, deep emotional healing can take place quickly in the astral plane. In a two-hour class my students tell me they can heal grief that would have taken two years or more to process in therapy. I think deep healing happens quickly in the astral planes for a couple reasons. First of all, emotions and time are accelerated there. When we are in the astral planes we can manifest an astral temple in moments, we can convey thoughts quickly and easily and we can accomplish many years' of therapy in a matter of minutes. So time moves differently. Beyond that, when we are in the astral realms, everything is pure, we are filled with love and truth and there are no obstacles to accomplishing what needs to be done. True healing is about returning to God, being One with God where there is no illness, no emotional upheaval, no off-kilter thoughts or feelings. Healing takes place quickly. Remember how much easier it was for me to stay out of body then return to my physical body during my NDE? That is because our physical bodies are altered, they are not pure God, they are not pure health, and they are not pure love. Our astral or spiritual bodies are God energy. When we are in the astral planes we resonate deeply with God's pure energy, then the astral body comes back and teaches the physical body how to heal.

I spend time in the astral realms daily communing with God and so I was able to release my grief in a prompt manner. I do of course miss waking up next to Michael every morning but I am ready for life to move on as God guides me on my path.

I know Michael is with me every day. Thank you Michael, for letting me know you are looking out for me.

Twenty-one
Medicine of the Future

*"What begins in the imagination becomes real - even though
that reality is of a different order than the reality
of the physical senses. It is the reality of the underlying
energy currents that shape the Universe."*
Michael Van Atta, January 4, 2003.

Can it be that there are "helpers" on the other side of the veil that motivate us to interact with others; orchestrating the right people to come together at the right time and then create positive change in the world? Maybe you remember an experience when you looked back at an event in your life and you realized it was kismet – the pre-determined integration of time, space and Divinely- inspired sharing of thoughts. Since Michael's death he has communicated to me that he is working on the other side to help those of us that are "in body" to realize how to morph cancerous cells into healthy ones.

Possibly, divine communication such as this is what happened with the writing of the Declaration of Independence. How about Martin Luther King? Was he channeling directly from God when he gave his "I Have a Dream" speech? It was certainly life-changing. Looking back on a Remote Viewing workshop that Michael and I taught in Colorado in 2009, it seems that there were greater forces at work. Maybe we were chess pieces being moved around to create a web or net of the right people coming together at the right time sharing ideas and talents.

The weekend workshop was initiated by Melvin Morse, MD. Melvin, a pediatrician, was well known for his many books including *Closer to the Light* and *Parting Visions.* Melvin had worked on a flight-for-life helicopter that was dispatched when children were on the verge of dying from severe traumas.

Melvin had the forethought to begin documenting children that came back to life through his involvement. Within the process of saving the lives of many children he heard similar stories recounted by the children about where they went and what they experienced when they were out of their bodies. I was excited to be his teacher since I had firsthand knowledge of the afterlife. Melvin was quite famous and had appeared on the Oprah Winfrey Show, Larry King Live and had been featured in Rolling Stone magazine. In the area of Near Death Experience studies, he was a household name. I found Melvin to be an intelligent and eccentric man with an eye to the future of medicine.

Dr. Morse approached my husband about a workshop in Remote Viewing. Michael had been the chairman of the Remote Viewing Club of

Denver, Colorado since 2001 and I believe Melvin had found him through the internet.

Melvin wanted to personally select who would be in the workshop, as he had a dream of advancing medicine though the incorporation of Remote Viewing. He chose Lance Beem, a plant biologist and bioscience researcher from California, who is now the owner of Beem Biologics. Lance met Melvin through Dannion Brinkley, author of *Saved By The Light*. Lance's daughter passed away through a tragic accident. He had some extraordinary experiences regarding contact with his daughter after she crossed over which prompted him to reach out to Damien.

Debra Katz, a professional psychic, was also invited. She filled the intuition role that Melvin wanted in the mix. Debra lives in California and has written many books including *You Are Psychic*, and *Extraordinary Psychic*. She regularly teaches classes to help others develop their psychic skills.

Melvin filled the role as a traditional medical professional and his wife, Pauline – a homemaker – also attended.

Michael and I were the instructors. Michael with his military background and Remote Viewing training from David Morehouse and me as an intuitive and Remote Viewer trained by Michael.

We were an interesting group. There was a lot of innovative discussion that took place between teachings. Melvin's goal was to advance current medical protocols to incorporate intuition or Remote Viewing to diagnose diseases. He had a vision of early diagnosis for diseases such as Hepatitis C and HIV so that they could be treated before there was a need for drugs such as interferon. At the time we taught this workshop, Interferon was the drug of choice to treat Hepatitis C and those who were prescribed that drug suffered extreme side effects.

As of the date of publication of this book, HIV is still not curable. In the United States an estimated .05 to .09 percent of the population are infected. There was some success with two babies who were treated with innovative drug protocols but one of them has once again tested positive. Antiretroviral therapy is the best thing available at this time. There has been some success with lowering the viral load within the blood to an amount that is not detectable however, that is not considered a cure as the viral load can fluctuate and increase at a later date. Also the use of chemical compounds to treat any illness causes its own issues. Prescribed manmade drugs is an unnatural alteration of the body chemistry manifesting in side effects that are sometimes more life threatening or debilitating than the disease being treated. Current common side effects of HIV/AIDS drugs include bone loss and heart disease.

Any disease would be easier to cure if the diagnosis could be made before it has taken a formidable hold on the physiology of the person. Melvin had a vision that if a patient could be scanned by a psychic or Remote Viewer checking the energy signature of a body and diagnose illness at an early stage that many illnesses currently considered to be life-threatening might be diagnosed early enough to be treatable without the use of abusive pharmaceuticals. Early diagnosis could make an alteration of diet or lifestyle the cure instead of extreme chemical alteration. Hepatitis C as well as AIDS are just a couple of illnesses that demand extreme measures once the symptoms are readily apparent. If there could be an earlier diagnosis, then the illness could be treatable and many lives would be saved. With this vision in mind, the plant virus study was born.

After the weekend concluded, the five of us worked on an initial plant virus experiment. Here is the protocol as it was set up.

The Core Group -
Preliminary Experiments
(excerpts from the study that was presented by Debra Katz at the IRVA conference 2010)

In May, 2009, a core group of researches interested in discovering and improving Remote Viewing applications in real life settings came together for the purpose of 1) Investigating whether remote viewing could be utilized to describe the structure of a microscopic organism such as a virus; and 2) Discovering whether it might be a useful diagnostic tool in medical application for determining the efficacy and timing of treatments applied to those suffering from viruses such as HIV or Hepatitis.

Eight tomato plants were grown in similar soil conditions, with similar water nutrients and light. One half of the plants were infected with the RNA Tobacco Mosaic Virus. The plants were divided into two groups and each group was assigned twenty-five random target numbers. So there were a total of fifty target numbers. The five initial viewers followed a military type of Remote Viewing protocol to view which plants were infected with the virus and which ones were not. Within the Remote Viewing process, as aspects of the target were reported on paper, at least two of the viewers were able to actually draw and describe the structure of the virus.

Our job as Remote Viewers was to connect to each target number and view the plants remotely to determine if there was evidence of a virus. This was a preliminary experiment to see if trained Remote Viewers could show a better percentage of accuracy than non-trained viewers.

Once this preliminary experiment was completed, it was decided that there was enough evidence of success to take the program to the next level. Further trials were run by varying the protocols. The first of those involved six viewers working fifty targets from different geographical locations but at the same time of day. This first protocol had an accuracy rate of 56% to 68%. This was a tedious three-hour process to complete the viewings with the protocols in place. I remember working these targets and it was not interesting, the repetition was monotonous and felt like drudgery. Certainly it was not as inspiring as traveling to the Holy of Holies. Apparently I was not the only one who felt that way according to what was written in the report.

"Viewers reported fatigue which lead to instances of guessing instead of following protocol. The research sample of fifty targets in one sitting was too large for the average volunteer."

As a healer, I was also struggling with the fact that healthy plants had been infected to benefit our experiments. I felt the distress of the plants. I struggled with the initial stages of the experiments. Also, because I was running my insurance agency, I did not have the time to invest in the further studies that took place. I am happy that my colleagues did continue as this is how progress advances. Thank goodness there are those out there that can move past or rise above or are oblivious to the communication that I feel with plants or other living things to advance our society.

Other issues considered were that the viewers were not getting immediate feedback on their viewings so they were not able to build on successes (remember the boxes that Michael used to train us, which immediately revealed our successes or weaknesses?)

From eight separate experiments it was found that Remote Viewers were successful in observing microscopic virus targets. By modifying the Binary Protocol (a yes-or-no identifying infection) and making some changes in the methodology the success rate could be increased based on motivation and incentive.

The study moved forward testing additional protocols. In total, twenty-three viewers completed 819 trials with a 60.68% accuracy rate.

In a professional paper that Melvin later published along with Michael and others it was reported:

"Regarding one of the studies done, showed that after 500 attempts (fifty viewings each for ten viewers) by non-trained people there was a 51.2% accuracy. For trained Remote Viewers the statistics were better, seven trained viewers achieved a 69.14% accuracy rate."

Within this professional paper the research question was presented:

Can humans use intuition, defined as the nonlocal acquisition of knowledge, in the form of remote viewing, to accurately identify whether or not a tomato plant is infected with the tobacco mosaic virus? If so, 1) Is there a specific protocol or remote viewing process which has the best results and 2) Can we improve intuition in viewers by changing protocol parameters, and in turn show that Intuition can (be) scientifically scrutinized?

There were five different viewing protocols for this particular test sample. Melvin's conclusion on this paper states:

The best results were obtained by persons experienced at remote viewing, two-person teams encouraged to communicate, and a previously described protocol which emphasized meditation, right-brain thinking, engaging the sensory stream of consciousness, an emotional connection to the target and visualizations.

I know when I worked on the tomato-plant virus targets in the early stages I was upset about the need to infect healthy plants with a virus. I tried my best to stay neutral or to connect to an energy of "buy-in" for the greater good. This was a baby step to advance medical science in a direction I was inspired by. It felt good to be on the ground floor of an innovative project such as this one but I also struggled with the deliberate infection of living plants.

There were five different protocols used and each time the protocol changed there was an increase of success in the viewing rates. Successes reached as high as 72.9%. This was quite impressive for a beginning study of revolutionary focus.

The conclusion of the professional paper reveled these insights:

Our results gave insight into the nature of intuition as also being a horizontal left-right brain process. The most successful protocol involved right-brain tasks such as engaging the sensory stream of consciousness, making an emotional connection with the target, using meditation to facilitate accessing the intuitive knowledge, and coupled with dialogue with a third party, to come up with a quick non-rational impression. This is very similar to descriptions of how intuition is best used by health- care professionals to make good clinical decisions.

The results also support our hypothesis that intuition is a complex process ultimately involving both hemispheres of the brain. The simplistic Protocols 2 and 3 which had ritualistic and superstitious elements in them were not significant from the null hypothesis results. As more complexity was added to the process, experience, meditation, communication with a partner and an emphasis on information for the right brain, there was an increasingly significant success.

This study provides a basis for future research to build on our results and our theory of consciousness and intuition. Intuition is part of a complex feedback system embedded in Top Down Causation. Although seemingly instantaneous, it is actually a simultaneous unfolding of a complex array of cognitive and physiological changes in response to the novel information. The truly simplistic efforts at nonlocal perception involving a quick guess, a ritualistic tapping on a sketch of the target, or simply asking the plant if it was infected did not result in a significant acquisition of non-local information.

This study demonstrates that intuition is not a form of mystical insight but can be studied using scientific methods.

As a result of this trial run, a grant was eventually awarded to the group to do further studies. The award, the René Warcollier Prize, was awarded by IRVA, the International Remote Viewing Association. Rene' Warcollier was a French parapsychologist that some refer to as the father of Remote Viewing. The award was dedicated to Michael and the study went on to be recognized in Helsinki, Finland. Over a three-year period, the study was considered the largest of its kind, far exceeding any project that involved Remote Viewing by the U. S. military.

As this book nears publication, the paper has been submitted to the Journal of Scientific Exploration. They are conducting a peer review to decide if they want to publish it.

Who knows where this preliminary study will lead in advancing modern medical science? Will a merging of intuition and science eventually be used as an accepted manner of diagnostic techniques? Or could it be that our mainstream doctors are already incorporating some intuition in their diagnostic processes without actually acknowledging it?

Within our typical viewings, Michael and I did not follow strict military protocols. Our teaching style of Remote Viewing incorporated many of the techniques but also included energetic protection to shield the viewers from emotional distress and other features that were not strict military protocols. However, there were some profound things that came out of that long weekend workshop.

*Debra, Lance, Melvin and his wife all gained a beginning-level exposure to the process of Remote Viewing. All of them went on to learn the more strict military protocols taught by Lyn Buchanan.

*The Kari Beem Foundation was created in honor of Lance's daughter with the following goals:

1) To help grieving parents understand that their spiritual visions, intuitions, and dreams are real and can facilitate healing.

2) To understand the practical lessons of near-death experiences, creating medical applications for remote viewing, and new therapies for autism, post-traumatic stress syndrome, and the human soul.

More information on the foundation can be found at:

www.beemoflight.com/html/contact.html

*The plant virus study later was developed and documented in a professional paper written by Melvin L. Morse, MD; John Peter Thompson; Stephan A Schwartz; Lance Willam Beem, MS; Debra Katz MSW; Angela Ronson, MA; and Michael Van Atta, titled *A Qualitative Study of the Nonlocal Processes of Intuition Using Remote Viewing Protocols.*

*Michael and I were introduced to the Random Event Generator (REG) by Melvin Morse.

The REG was developed by Princeton University and is computer software that produces 1's and 0's. The premise of the Random Event Generator is that any energy within a space is typically random until there is a change or shift of energy. This shift can take place by alteration and coherence of thought, emotion, or energy within a space. When we encouraged students to focus on the same target number and explore the aspects of the target, their thought processes could alter the energy within the space from random to uniformity. This shift is reflected on a computer screen in graph form. Even more interesting, Princeton University conducted experiments showing that the consciousness of humans on our planet can alter energy from randomness to uniformity in advance of a major event such as an earthquake or the 9/11 attack. It can document the energy of the premonition to a significant event.

Michael and I began to use the REG when working in tandem on Reiki clients as well as when we worked Remote Viewing targets. Melvin Morse posted a video on YouTube showing him working a Remote Viewing target on a plant virus study while the REG is monitoring the lack of randomness (or evidence of uniformity or coherence) within his field. That video can be viewed at https://www.youtube.com/watch?v= Y2Xdm7O4W8M

What will medicine of the future look like? Will science and metaphysics finally combine to utilize the best of both to advance healing in the future? I am honored to have been included in the baby steps of this research. Projecting the possibilities into the future, being able to sense a virus of

Hepatitis C, AIDS, Cancer, and other deadly issues in their stages of infancy could save the medical system millions of dollars and improve the lives of those on our planet. The cost of health insurance, medications and other areas of our traditional medical model would be greatly reduced. It may take decades for this program or any other similar program to be accepted by the cultures of our planet but it does instill hope that there are extraordinary minds who are willing to think outside of normal parameters to advance our ways of thinking and conducting our lives.

Imagine the doctor's office of the future. Instead of blood tests, X-rays and MRI's to evaluate why you are not feeling well, you are sent into a quiet room with meditation music and dim lighting and a skilled Remote Viewer scans energy field to find any areas that have blockages and may contain viruses. With this program in place the technician would even be able to identify what type of virus was present and due to early detection, the reversal of the issue would be less expensive, less invasive and the success rate of cure would be far greater. Also the emotional toll that an advanced serious diagnosis takes on the individual as well as his or her family will be far less. We owe the military for bringing Remote Viewing into the mainstream and giving it validation.

Twenty-two
Crystal Clear Communication

"Love is the glue of the universe."
Marcel Vogel

"All healing is a consequence of loving."
Rumi Da

As time progressed, living with Michael was like living in Disneyland for psychic alternative-healing adults. Our home was filled with Radionics experiments, crystal arrays laid out on the floor in mandala patterns to enter for meditation, plant communication experiments, labyrinths, aura meters, aura photography devices and other interesting items. Michael and I together were constantly striving to improve our abilities by exploring the unseen, energetic world. I consider this the God-scape. The more connected to God, the more we developed our healing and psychic abilities.

Here is one of the experiments that we used to enhance our abilities. We purchased two Vogel-cut crystals. Vogel-cut crystals are typically clear quartz which is a mineral, known for its properties of having the ability to be programmed. The Vogel-cut is named after scientist, Marcel Vogel. He has been attributed to producing more than 100 patents and advances in the area of luminescence. Marcel was the IBM scientist who developed the liquid crystal diode for the color television.

Rumi Da, spiritual mentor, who became good friends with him, stated that Marcel told him,

"When I was between the ages of five and eight years old I was watching TV and this strange character named Elmer Fudd came on dressed up like a swami, wearing a turban and staring into a crystal ball. And I remember looking at him and saying to myself, "That is what I want to be when I grow up."

In developing the liquid crystal diode, Marcel realized the crystals would form differently based on what he was thinking or feeling. There was communication taking place between him and the crystals – quite a profound observation for this scientist.

Marcel continued to do experiments with crystals and wanted to standardize the energetic process so it could be measured. In working with quartz crystals, he realized that the energy emitted varied greatly depending on the quality of the crystal as well as how it was cut into facets. Wanting to standardize the process for experiments, he meditated on the best cut for a crystal to be used for communication and received the vision of the Kabalistic Tree of Life.

From this meditation, a crystal was formed in the shape of a faceted cylinder with tapered pointes at each end mimicking the Tree of Life symbol. This cut became known as a Vogel-cut crystal. It is interesting that the angles on the Tree of Life are not in coherence with the natural cleaving angles of a quartz crystal, which makes the Vogel-cut crystal quite fragile.

Quartz crystals have been proven to have special properties of 1) storing information, 2) broadcasting information. Newsweek published an article in September, 1994, about Stanford Research Institute scientists placing a three-dimensional image of the Mona Lisa into a quartz crystal and then retrieving it. Crystals were used in early radios and today crystal or silicon technology is used in our computers.

From the website, www.spiritofmaat.com:

The Vogel-cut crystal was created specifically to amplify and cohere the thought and energy that you wish to direct into your body/mind or that of another person.

Working with true Vogel-cuts that were purchased through Rumi Da, we began our experiments. After clearing our crystals, Michael and I did a series of experiments where one of us would program an image into their crystal. That Vogel-cut crystal would communicate with the other one and the receiving person would pick up the image from their crystal.

As we did these experiments, we documented what took place during the first set of trials.

Michael was at work, I was working at home that day. While out jogging, I got the message in my brain, "You've got mail." When I got home, I picked up my Vogel-cut crystal and entered an altered brainwave state to receive the information. Here is an excerpt of an email from me to Michael:

I see a male deer, a buck, with large antlers. I see him shaking his head back and forth.

The scene played in my mind's eye like a movie. Michael immediately wrote back to me in email:

Target was a live male mule deer with antlers, moving his head.

Another time, I envisioned a new video within my crystal and emailed this to him:

I just picked up a vision from my Vogel-cut crystal. It is like a key, not a living thing. I see it as metal, part round, part elongated and flat.

Michael's email back to me stated:

The target was an access badge allowing card-key access through doors in a secured building. It is attached to a pull clip that is black and circular and has a metal clip for one to hook the badge on their belt. The badge itself is a long slender magnetic card that acts as a key when pressed against a red light at the door and the door opens.

I don't think I did as well on that target but you could say I did get some "hits." Michael and I did many more transmissions. After many trials with him as the transmitter and me as the

188

receiver, we switched places. I am not sure why but we did not do as well that way. I was a better receiver and he was a better transmitter. We did approximately fourteen of these experiments, clearing our crystals each time we completed a session.

You are most likely already transmitting and receiving thought forms on a daily basis. Sometimes you may not even be aware that it is happening. You think of a friend right before the phone rings and they are the one who is calling you. Or maybe you wake up in the middle of the night thinking about your sister to find out the next morning that she was in a car accident. Creating an awareness of these events and not discounting them can help you to advance your skills to the next level. The use of crystals within this work simply enhances your abilities.

Marcel Vogel passed away in 1991. He came to me a few times in my dreams, showing me a meditation chamber made entirely of quartz crystals.

I continue to use my Vogel-cut crystal in my Reiki healing practice.

Twenty-three
A Letter to Michael

*Offering hope to another is the
embodiment of the Holy Spirit.*
Michael Mirdad, March 2016.

I enter an altered state of brain waves by focusing on my breath. Deep, deep inhale, long slow exhale. Deep, deep inhale, long slow exhale. Moving the darkness out, filling with golden light of the Divine. Breathing in, blowing out... a few more times. Clearing my mind.

Focusing on the astral address, I send my consciousness there, entering our astral temple as I have done so many times before. I sense Michael's energy signature around me as if he is already there waiting for me. We settle in together, comingling energies as we have done so very many times before. I feel melancholy as I do this. I know it is time to let go; time to move on. I know I need to live my life and to let go of the past and hanging onto Michael's spirit is the main thing holding me back.

Through my thoughts and my emotions I fill the space with the energy of all that I am; appreciation and gratitude, love and friendship, respect and honoring, regrets of words not spoken to him while he was in body. I know it is time for some closure and time to change channels and move forward. I ask Michael for his blessing in my choosing to enter into a new relationship. He tells me he is the one who has orchestrated this new love interest that I am connected to. The new guy is spiritual, humorous, affectionate, sensual, intelligent, good looking. He is filled with God energy. Michael knows that. Michael knows what is important to me. He knows what I need in a man. I am in an energy field of renewed hope and gratitude. I feel deep unspeakable emotions. I am blessed and divinely guided.

Meeting Michael was a gift from God. Meeting my new guy is a gift from Michael and from God. I release Michael to the work he is meant to continue on the other side; helping healers find out that they are healers and helping them to develop cancer research.

He has touched me deeply and left a mark on my life that will be there forever; an astral tattoo of sorts. I am free to move forward. I have no lack in my life. I am Divinely guided. I am blessed.

Thank-you Michael, for all that you taught me and for becoming one of my spirit guides, always there to watch over me and protect me. Thank you for restoring hope into my heart and into my life. You have blessed my life.

With Love,
Luna Star Van Atta
March 13, 2016.

Epilogue
Remote Viewing
My Near Death Experience

Journal Entry September, 2012

I leave my body with the intent to access a target which I call "NDE Purpose." I want to Remote View the soul signature of my Near Death Experience, the energy of the adventure. I want more information as to why it even happened. In accessing the target, I receive the following information.

You are one with God, you are a healer of emotional blockages. The people who come to you will have changed lives because you touched them on a very deep level, and cleared away their pain. I helped you come into this body and to experience these pains, emotional pains so that you would be able to help others and to mold them into a higher frequency. You had many other lifetimes as a healer and you were also groomed during this lifetime to move into this role. You are an opener of doorways, a clearer of blockages. A person may be from another dimension or another planet, and any life you have touched has changed you and you have changed all of it for the better. Even though it did not feel like that at the time, you moved into the role as a healer, counselor and intuitive without making a decision, it all just came to you unannounced, snuck up on you, unassuming, hiding in the shadows and you became aware of the impact and how it would change your life. Many people come to you now for guidance for messages and for healing. You help them to see the light, to be enlightened and that is your true gift to enlighten others, to bring the light into their realms, into their worlds. Your heart radiates outward and glows with the energy of the creator. When this happens the energy that is glowing, flowering outward, touches others and so when you heal one heart, you actually heal more than that because there is a rippling effect that takes place, moving outward in concentric circles. Those circles carry the energy of healing and that energy is moved outward to others.

Bibliography

Bach, Richard. *Illusions, The Adventures of a Reluctant Messiah.* Dell Publishers. 1989.

Brennan, J.H. *The Astral Projection Workbook,* Sterling, 1989.

Brinkley, Dannion. *Saved by the Light.* Harper Collins Publishers. 1994.

Bruce, Robert. *Astral Dynamics.* Hampton Roads Publishing Company, VA. 1999.

Buhlman, William. *Adventures Beyond the Body.* Harper Collins Publishers, Inc. 1996.

Denning, Melita and Osborne Phillips. *The Llewellyn Practical Guide to Astral Projection.* St Paul, MN. Llewellyn Worldwide, 1979

Dispenza, Joe D.C., *Evolve Your Brain.* Health Communications, Inc. 2007.

Fu, Chung. *Under the Plum Tree, The Tao of Everything.* Inkwell: Dobbins, CA. 2002

Gilbert, Elizabeth. *Eat, Pray, Love.* Penguin Books, LTD, London. 2006.

Katz, Debra. *Extraordinary Psychic.* Llewellyn Productions. 2008

Monroe, Robert. *Far Journeys.* Doubleday, Garden City, NY. 1985

_____. *Journeys Out-Of-Body.* Anchor Press, Garden City, NY. 1975.

_____. *The Ultimate Journey.* Doubleday, New York. 1994.

Morehouse, David. *Psychic Warrior.* St Martin Press, N.Y. 1996

Morse, Melvin L., John Peter Thompson, Stephan A Schwartz, Lance William Beem MS, Debra Katz MSW, Angela Ronson MA, Michael Van Atta. *A Qualitative Study of the Nonlocal Processes of Intuition Using Remote Viewing Protocols.*

Muldoon, Sylvan and Hereward Carrington. *The Projection of the Astral Body.* New York: Samuel Weiser, 1970. (Originally published in 1929).

Morse, Melvin, M.D. et al. *A Qualitative Study of the Nonlocal Processes of Intuition Using Remote Viewing Protocols.* Published Professional Paper. 2010.

Ophiel. *The Art and Practice of Astral Projection.* Samuel Weiser, New York, 1961.

Rumi Da., The Power of Crystals: The Legacy of Marcel Vogel. www.spiritofmatt.com/archive/mar1/vogel.htm, February, 2016

Solomon, Clavdius. Translated by S. Liddell Mac Gregor Mathers. *The Key of Solomon the King.* Samuel Weiser, Inc. ME. 1972.

The Denver Post, Thompson Charges, Verdicts. September 28, 2009

Tompkins, Peter and Christopher Bird. *The Secret Life of Plants.* Harper & Row Publishers, Inc. N.Y. 1973.

Wauters, Ambika. *The Book of Chakras,* Quarto Inc, 2002.

Van Atta, Michael. *http://lcweb2.loc.gov/frd/tfrussia/tfrhtml/tfr_report18th.html* Web page detailing Task Force Russia report showing Michael Van Atta testifying behind closed doors about Soviet involvement with American POW's.

Van Atta, Michael. Summit Independent Press, Summit, NJ 1992 two articles with photos of three Soviet Generals meeting in Russia with Michael Van Atta exchanging Soviet prisoner for American prisoners.

Van Atta, Michael. US House Resolution (HCR129) 1985, establishment of independent Perot Commission to determine if prisoners of war were being held in Indo-China and what action would be taken to get them out.

Van Atta, Michael. *http://www.gpo.gov/fdsys/pkg/ CRI-1986/html/CRI-1986-PICKLE-J-J-6A3D96.htm* web page of Congressional Record Index 1986. Perot Commission on Americans Missing in Southeast Asia. Perot's Commission produced a secret report that was still classified at the time that Michael wrote his "Fabric of Reality" list for me. Michael was one of the key men in the implementation of the Perot Commission.

Van Atta, Michael. 1990 testimony by Michael Van Atta as an expert witness at the U.S. Congressional committee on POW/MIA's in Washington, DC. regarding missing Americans in the Soviet Union; American prisoners as well as Soviet prisoners missing in Afghanistan. Michael provided hard copy documents from eye-witnesses in CIA and DIA files.

Van Atta, Michael. 1996 and 1997 Michael was one of the keynote speakers at the Special Forces Association's annual convention on missing Americans.

Van Atta, Michael and Luna (Susan) and Morse Melvin. *Controlled Remote Viewing for Scientific Investigations.* Sacred Mountain Sanctuary. 2009.

Varga, Josie, *Visits to Heaven, 4th Dimension Press, VA, 2010.*

Walsch, Neale Donald. *Conversations with God.* G.P. Putnam, NY. 1995

www.abouthealth.com April 11, 2016

www.missingkids.org. September 12, 2015

www.spiritofmaat.com January 10, 2016

www.webmd.com April 7, 2016

www.youtube.com January 5, 2016

www.ingramcontent.com/pod-product-compliance
Lightning Source LLC
LaVergne TN
LVHW011225080426
835509LV00005B/325